To:_____

From:_____

Dedications

–from Angie:

For my girls: Ellie, Abby, Kate, Audrey, and Charlotte. Being your mommy is one of the greatest gifts God has ever given me, and I thank Him every day for allowing me the privilege. I love you so, so much.

–from Breezy:

To my wonderful father and mother, for faithfully teaching me the truths of Scripture, and to my sister, Emily Rose, for her boundless friendship and support. I'm so thankful to the Lord for each of you.

Scripture quotations are taken from the Holman Christian Standard Bible®,
Copyright © 1999, 2000, 2002, 2003, 2009 by Holman Bible Publishers.
Also used: The Holy Bible, English Standard Version (ESV), copyright © 2001
by Crossway Bibles, a publishing ministry of Good News Publishers.

Dewey Decimal Classification: J220.95
Subject Heading: GIRLS \ BIBLE STORIES \ WOMEN IN THE BIBLE

ISBN: 978-1-4336-8046-5
Printed in China
1 2 3 4 5 6 7 8 - 18 17 16 15 14

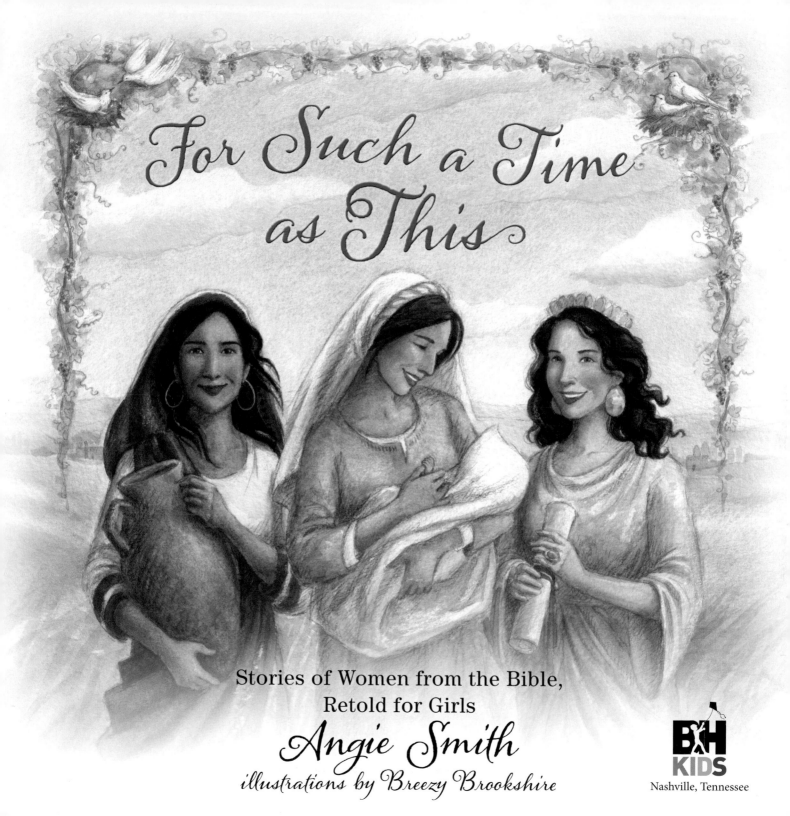

For Such a Time as This

Stories of Women from the Bible, Retold for Girls

Angie Smith

illustrations by Breezy Brookshire

B&H KIDS

Nashville, Tennessee

A Letter to Parents

One of the joys of having a daughter is watching her uncover the exciting story God has written for her life. The more she knows about God's Word, the more likely she is to let its truths guide her decisions and shape her character. That's the purpose of *For Such a Time as This*, a Bible storybook where today's girls can learn invaluable lessons from the biblical women of yesterday—lessons about perseverance, obedience, and faith. Together, their lives tell a greater story of the Bible itself.

To help girls connect more directly and deeply with the stories, each one ends with a unique "He, Me, She" section.

- The "He" section focuses on God and highlights a facet of His character that was revealed in the story. Here girls can get to know God better.

- The "Me" section focuses on the reader and explains how girls can incorporate the truth of each story into their daily lives. What new character traits can they pursue?

- The "She" section is written for the parents and offers a Scripture-based prayer they can pray over their daughter.

You will also find a memory verse that relates to the story and a Hebrew or Greek word for you to learn together as a family. I welcome you to jump in and make this story time an enjoyable part of your day together, a time for your family to connect with each other and with God.

My hope is that our girls will see that these are not just Bible stories but *our stories*. They are stories of great mercy and grace that make up the history of our faith, and they were put here to guide our daughters through their own walks of faith, passed down to them for such a time as this.

–Angie

Remember

*Your eyes saw me when I was formless; all my days were written in Your book
and planned before a single one of them began.—Psalm 13:16*

Read

Read 2 Timothy 1:3–7; 3:14–15. These verses tell us a bit about two other women in the Bible: Lois and Eunice, the grandmother and mother of Timothy. They taught Timothy to love God and His Word from the time he was a little boy, so He grew up to be a great missionary and share the love of Jesus far and wide. Just like Lois and Eunice, you can teach other people about Jesus too—He will use your life to share His love.

Think

1. These Bible women lived a long, long time ago and in a place that is much different than where most of us live. Why are their stories still important?

2. If you had to pick one of these women as a role model, which would you pick? Why?

3. Some of these stories are about women who sinned and did not put God first in their lives. Why do you think God included their stories in the Bible too?

4. Think about some of the character traits you learned from these biblical women. Pick one trait each week and try to grow it and show it in your daily life.

5. Did these stories teach you more about what God is like? If an unbelieving friend asked you to describe your God, what would you say?

6. How does it feel when you hear your parents say a prayer for you? Next time they pray for you, surprise them and say a prayer for them too.

7. Pretend you are writing a story about the rest of your life. Who would be in it? What would happen? Could girls who one day read the story learn lessons from your life about how to live for Jesus?

***God has already written your story, and He has exciting plans for you,
His cherished daughter!***

For more Parent Connection ideas and activities, visit us at BHKidsBuzz.com.

Stories of Women from the Bible

The Garden

The Story of Eve

She was made for him, no question.
   Where there was once a rib in Adam's chest, there was now a scar reminding them both of the way God had made her. You see, God didn't want Adam to live all alone, so He took a part from Adam and shaped and molded it into the very first bride the world had known: Eve.

Adam loved her in an instant. She was as much a part of him then as his very rib had been. Life together was barefoot and perfect, every moment a gift from the Giver. God saw them running, jumping, laughing, and full of His breath. It was just the way God wanted it to be.

They were free to live in His amazing creation and could enjoy anything around them.

With one exception . . .

God told them not to eat the fruit from one specific tree in the garden, and He warned them that if they disobeyed there would be terrible consequences.

The days spilled one into another until one afternoon Eve found herself near the tree. A voice, gentle as rain, asked her a question that would change everything.

Shhh. Listen . . . .

"Are you sure He said you couldn't eat from this tree?" Satan was clothed as a serpent, living in the garden. He was eager to steal the glory of God. What better way than to persuade God's own creation to betray Him?

The serpent told Eve that the fruit would make her wise. And as her eyes followed the striking outline of the branches, she could think of nothing else but tasting that fruit.

Why wouldn't God want her to be wise?

Fingers cupped around the fruit, she pressed her lips to the curse of death. It was sweet for a moment, as rebellion often is. Adam ate the fruit as well, and they both knew right away that they had made a terrible choice.

As the wind rustled the dry leaves, they tried to cover themselves out of shame. For the first time, they understood how scary it was to disobey such a powerful God.

Can you imagine? One moment. One decision. It changed everything. And there was no going back now.

God sent Adam and Eve out of the place that had always been home. As they wandered far from the garden, I wonder if they could hear the anguish in God's voice: *This wasn't what I wanted for you . . . .*

Her mistake was too big to be fixed by human hands, but many years later, another Man would be wounded for her and for all of those who believe in Him. If God had wanted to, He could have separated Himself from them (and us) forever, but He didn't.

Even as He sent Adam and Eve away, God knew that one day He would make a way to bring them back to Him.

—FROM GENESIS 3

He

God is **sovereign**, the highest ruler of all, and nothing can happen unless He allows it. He is in control of everything, and everything depends on Him, including us.

God gave people free will, which means we can make our own decisions. Sometimes we make good ones, and other times we don't.

Sin is an action, a thought, or a decision that goes against God. Because of the first sin in the garden, everyone would be sinful, including you and me. So why did God allow Eve to sin? He could have stopped her, and then everything would have stayed perfect forever!

Remember, He has a plan we can't see. And even though this wasn't what He wanted, He allowed it to happen because He knows the whole story, and this was a part of it. We are going to learn more and more about His story as we read and about the amazing way He rescued us. But we'll get to that soon enough!

Me

Obedience is when we keep the rules and commands of God and of people who are in charge of us. It is important that we are obedient because it keeps us from harm and shows others that we have respect for them. God tells us to be obedient to our parents in Colossians 3:20: "Children, obey your parents in everything, for this pleases the Lord."

She

Lord, help _Faith_ to be obedient in all things. When she is tempted to disobey, remind her that there is a better way that will lead to righteousness (Romans 6:16) and the purification of her soul (1 Peter 1:22). Give her the strength to stand firm when she sees others being disobedient and the courage to make the right decisions based on what she knows of You. Father, I come to You because I know how fickle my own heart is and how easily my thoughts wander from You. Remind me to set my mind on Your Spirit instead of my own flesh so that I will have peace and will please You by submitting to Your law (Romans 8:5–8). And help me to delight in Your law in my inner being (Romans 7:22) so that I may lead her in a way that models obedience.

Tsavah (tsah VAH) is the Hebrew word for "command."
The memory verse for this story is Genesis 1:1—
"In the beginning, God created the heavens and the earth."

Window of Heaven

The Story of Noah's Wife

Thud.

Thud.

Thud.

Noah's wife watched as he hammered,
her eyes shining with love for him.

She had watched day after day as he
worked on the boat that God had commanded him to build.
Despite the lack of rain and the mocking of the crowds gathered
around him, he would continue until it was time to climb inside.

He would do exactly what God told him to,
down to the very measurements of the boat.

God had been so kind, so patient with His rebellious creation.
But the world had become a terrible place where people did whatever they wanted. They loved themselves more than the God who
gave them breath. They turned their backs, shook their heads, and
laughed at the idea of God's power.

But not Noah.

As his wife watched Noah's hands move from side-to-side across the
boat, his brow wet with sweat, she thanked her heavenly Father for him.
God had chosen her husband, Noah, a righteous man, to be the one to
build the boat. He would build for decades, until it stood high above the
earth, with nothing more than God's promises to cling to in his old age.

One day, Noah whispered the words she had anticipated for so long, and they climbed aboard, seeing the inside of the boat with new eyes. According to God's command, they brought only their family: their three sons and their sons' wives. They had also been told to bring seven pairs of each kind of clean animal, one pair of each kind of unclean animal, and seven pairs of each kind of bird. They did everything God had asked of them, even though a drop of rain hadn't yet fallen on their obedience.

She had heard Noah warning the people for years that a great flood was coming to tear their homes apart and destroy them, but they wouldn't listen. They chose death instead of life over and over again, and it grieved God terribly.

She could still hear the echo in her mind.

Thud. Thud. Thud.

Every day she had listened to the sound of hammers pounding, shaping the boat that would rescue them from death.

And now they were actually inside the boat, the "ark" Noah had built, trusting that the Lord would keep them safe. God told them that He would send the rain in seven days, and in seven days He did exactly that.

Drop, drop, drop . . .

The fountains of the great deep burst forth, the window of heaven opened, and the rain poured down. It slipped from high above and covered the ground. It swallowed the towns, the people, and everything that lived, and it didn't stop for forty days.

God kept His promise to Noah to save his family from the flood, and He painted the sky with another promise once they were safe on dry ground again. "The rainbow," God told them, "is a symbol to remind you that I will never flood the earth again."

Many, many years later, the sound of a hammer pounding would pierce the silence again, driving nails into the wood of a cross.

Thud. Thud. Thud.

While the crowds mocked Him, there would be women who knew what He was doing for God—what He was doing for them. Standing high above the ground, the cross would bring life instead of death. The window of heaven would open again, and scarlet-colored droplets would rain from high above. Jesus Himself would be hung to cleanse us, and the flood of mercy would make us right with Him forever.

Drop, drop, drop . . .

—FROM GENESIS 6–9

He

God's creation had sinned against Him, and as a result He had to punish them. We call this God's **judgment**. Does judgment mean God doesn't love His people? The truth is, He loves them so much that He can't stand to let them go on in such a wicked way. Even though He could have destroyed everything in His anger, He chose to let several people live to start things over again.

Noah was a **righteous** man, which meant that even though he wasn't perfect (none of us are!), he put God first and really tried to obey His rules.

After God destroyed the world in the flood, He made a promise to Noah that He would never do such a thing again. We can trust God, even in His judgment, because behind that punishment is always love.

Me

So many times we just want to do things our way. But God wants you to do things the way He created you to. He wants you to do what He says is right and good. The first step is admitting that you aren't the boss and telling Him that you want to do what He says is best. When you do this, you are showing **humility**, which means you realize that He knows you better than you know yourself.

She

Lord, help _Faith_ to learn the value of humility and give her a desire to do what is right in Your eyes. Help her as she goes about her day, and in every decision she makes, help her to see what You want her to do. As she studies Your Word, give her a deep understanding of Your love for her, and help her to know You as a loving Father who treasures her. Lord, help me to model humility and righteousness to her in a way that leads her into a solid faith and genuine understanding of You and Your Word.

Tsaddiyq (tsad DEEK) is the Hebrew word for "righteous."
The memory verse for this story is Genesis 9:1—
"Be fruitful and multiply and fill the earth."

Stars and Sons

The Story of Sarai

The night sky was dripping with stars, and Abram's head was tipped upward as God spoke to him.

"Count them if you can," God said. But Abram couldn't, of course; it was impossible.

"One day, you will have as many descendants—children, grandchildren, and on and on—as there are stars above you," God promised him.

How could it be? Abram was an old man, and his wife an old woman. They had never had children, and now it was too late. But Abram was a faithful man, and he believed God, even though he couldn't imagine it.

But when Abram told Sarai, she shook her head.

"God has never given me children," she answered, her fingers smoothing the gray hairs that danced around her head. She looked out into the night, considered her husband's words, and suggested the only thing that seemed to her to be a reasonable solution.

"Marry Hagar." She knew that her maid Hagar was young enough to have a baby, and Sarai and Abram could raise him as their own.

Where God saw a miracle, Sarai could only see her wrinkled reflection. Where He was making a way, she was making her own plan instead.

So Abram and Hagar married and had a son, whom they named Ishmael. But he wasn't the baby God had promised, and God spoke to Abram again.

"Abram, I am God Almighty, and I have made a promise to you. I am changing your name to Abraham because it means 'father of nations.'"

Abraham listened as God continued.

"Sarai will now be called Sarah," God continued, "and in a year she will have a son named Isaac."

God told Abraham of the kings that would come from this son and of the way Isaac's people would be special to God because of the promise He was making to Abraham.

Abraham fell to the ground in awe, and he laughed in joy at what God was going to do.

Sarah also laughed when she heard God's promise, but not because she was excited and happy. Instead, she was thinking of how ridiculous it would be for a baby to be born to a woman who was ninety years old.

More than just being ridiculous, she believed it was impossible.

Months later, Sarah held that promise in her arms. With the very same lips that had called him impossible, she kissed his head and whispered his name.

Isaac.

It meant "laughter," and Sarah would never forget the way she had laughed at God's plan, choosing her reflection over the chance to reflect Him.

"Count the stars, if you can," God had whispered, knowing that Abraham couldn't.

"She will have a son," He had said, knowing she should believe Him but she wouldn't.

As Sarah learned, nothing is too hard for God. His hands place stars and sons and everything in between, even when we are convinced it's impossible.

—FROM GENESIS 15

He

Just as He did with Noah, God makes a promise with Abraham too. Another word for promise is **covenant**. When God says He is going to do something, it isn't a "maybe." In fact, God cannot break His promises because it would go against everything that He is.

Sarah laughed when God promised that she would have a baby. I can imagine that she just couldn't see how God would use her because she was so old! But here's where we learn another important lesson about God: He loves to use weak people to show the world how strong He is.

Through Sarah, God was able to show everyone that He doesn't need our strength or qualifications to make His name known. In fact, sometimes they can get in the way.

Me

Trust is a hard thing, even when we can see and hear the person. In the case of God, we can't even see Him, and it can make that trust even harder. But when we read the Bible, we are reminded of how God showed up for His people time after time, and we can build our trust in Him. That's one reason it's so important to spend time reading God's Word. If He was there for all of those people in the Bible, you know that you can trust Him to be there when you need Him too.

She

Lord, I pray that as _____ lifts up her prayers to You, let her be reminded of the way You care for her and take her burdens on as Yours. Help her to know that You can work through her, even when she feels weak or fearful, and help her understand the power of trust. Give me words to teach her well, and strengthen my trust in You so that I am a living example of believing in You even when it seems impossible to me. Give me hope where I need it the most and the tools to pass along that hope to her in a way that makes You more real.

Bĕriyth (bear EETH) is the Hebrew word for "covenant."
The memory verse for this story is Genesis 17:4—"As for Me, My covenant is with you:
you will become the father of many nations."

The Well

The Story of Hagar

*I*t wasn't a question for her to answer—it was a command from Sarah for her to obey.

Hagar would marry Abraham.

As a handmaiden, Hagar belonged to her mistress, Sarah. She would marry Sarah's husband, as she was told, and have a child that Sarah could treat as her own. But after Hagar became pregnant, she began to act like more of an equal than a maidservant should.

As you can imagine, this did not go over well with Sarah. She made life miserable for Hagar by piling up duties and taking away privileges. So Hagar decided to run away. Pregnant and desperate, she fled into the wilderness to try and find a place where life would be easier.

It was a very difficult journey. When she stopped beside a well to rest, she heard a voice, and she knew it was God Himself. "Hagar, where are you going?" Of course He knew the answer, but He wanted her to consider it for herself.

"I have run away from my mistress, Sarah," Hagar answered, fully aware that she had no right to do such a thing.

"Go back to Sarah and obey her," God commanded. But seeing her sadness, He gave her a glimpse into what was to come. "Your son will be named Ishmael," God explained, telling her a bit of who he would become.

There beside a well, her belly swollen with child, Hagar was reminded that God had always been watching and always would be. She wasn't merely a maidservant to her mistress, but rather a maidservant to the Lord most high.

She returned to Sarah and Abraham and soon delivered the boy God had promised.

As Ishmael grew older, Hagar and Sarah still struggled for power, but one day everything changed. Against all odds, Sarah became pregnant. After Abraham and Sarah's son Isaac was born, she demanded that Abraham send Hagar and Ishmael away so that they wouldn't be a bad influence on her son.

Although it saddened him, Abraham did as Sarah asked. He rose early in the morning, packed food and water for Hagar and Ishmael, and said good-bye to them.

So Hagar left again, but this time it was because she was forced to go. As the desert stretched out before her and her son, their legs exhausted and their water supply long gone, Hagar began to doubt they would make it out alive.

Ishmael was near death, his body too weak to continue, so Hagar laid him under a bush and walked away from him, unable to watch her only son die while she stood helpless.

She wasn't thinking about the promises God had given her by the well years ago. Like Sarah, she could only see what was right in front of her.

Emptiness. No chance for life. Impossible.

Hagar closed her eyes in surrender and cried out in sadness. She couldn't provide water for her son anymore than she could count the stars in the sky. But that, after all, was exactly the point.

"Hagar," God whispered, "don't be afraid. Get up and help your son to stand; I am not finished with him yet."

God opened her eyes at that moment, and she looked around, seeing something she hadn't noticed before: a well of water.

Hagar had given up, closed her eyes, and missed the one thing that could bring life to her son. And God, in His mercy, showed her that He was taking care of her all along.

Barren wombs and barren deserts are simply opportunities for the Lord to remind us of our own weakness and His perfect strength.

In every word He spoke to Hagar, the message remained the same.

I see you.

My promises will stand as strong as your son; raise him up and walk in confidence, knowing that the words I spoke over you are as true as the water dripping into his mouth.

No matter where you've come from, no matter where you go, or what you've seen as impossible in your life, one thing remains: none of it was unseen by Me.

–FROM GENESIS 16; 21

He

God is **omnipresent**, which means He is everywhere at once. Even when we feel like we are all alone, we aren't. That's good news for the times when we are sad and lonely and feel like nobody cares about what's happening to us. He is with us! The next time you feel this way, remember that in that very moment, the God of the universe is with you, and He cares about the details of your life.

Me

Hope comes from knowing that we have a Father who is always taking care of us and has our best in mind. Even when things around you seem to be going wrong, remember that God is at work. Romans 8:28 says this: "We know that all things work together for the good of those who love God: those who are called according to His purpose."

She

Lord, help __Faith__ to sense Your presence in the times that she feels alone. Remind her in those moments that Your watchful eye is upon her and that she can call out to You from whatever desert she feels lost in. Speak courage and hope to her when she worries that she has been forgotten. Your Word declares this: "Be strong and courageous; don't be terrified or afraid of them. For it is the Lord your God who goes with you; He will not leave you or forsake you" (Deuteronomy 31:6). May I walk in the light of this promise and teach her to as well.

__Tiqvah__ (tik VAH) is the Hebrew word for "hope."
The memory verse for this story is Genesis 21:19—
"Then God opened her eyes, and she saw a well of water."

Pillar

The Story of Lot's Wife

Abraham's cousin Lot sat beside the city gate, watching people wander into the terrible city. Every time he heard the creaking of the gate, it meant more people had wandered in to be a part of all the terrible things that happened there.

When he saw two men coming in, he immediately knew that something was different about them.

"Please, lords, come to my house," Lot called to them. "The city is awful, and you don't need to be a part of these things. I'll give you some food and a warm bed, and you can avoid going any farther into this madness."

The men acted like they were just going to go ahead anyway, but Lot's voice grew more insistent.

"Please, I beg you. Come with me." He pointed toward his house and tried to push them in that direction.

Lot and his wife and children had lived in Sodom for some time, and they knew it was a place that had forgotten God. Everywhere they looked, there were people doing terrible things and living like they weren't worried about the consequences.

And Lot was right about these men: they weren't ordinary people. In fact, they were angels disguised as men who had been sent by God to see the horror for themselves.

Lot baked them warm bread and showed them where they could sleep, but before they lay down for the night there was a pounding on the front door.

"Send them out here!" the men of the city shouted. This was exactly what Lot was trying to protect them from—the evil men who wanted to hurt the strangers, to make sure they didn't stay pure in such a dirty place.

Lot stepped outside and begged the men of Sodom to leave, explaining that it didn't have to happen this way. But the crowds were determined, and they began to push Lot against the door in order to break in and take his guests.

In that moment, the angels pulled Lot inside, slamming the door shut. Then they made it so that all the people outside were blinded and stumbling around to try and find their way.

"Your wife. Get her," the angels said to Lot. "And the rest of your family as well. You have to get out of this city quickly because God is going to destroy it!"

Lot went outside to call the two men engaged to his daughters, but when they heard his warning they ignored him because they thought he was kidding.

By the time the sun rose the next morning, they were all still there. Lot's wife didn't seem to be in a great hurry either, even though he had warned her. Finally, out of mercy, the angels picked them up and brought them outside the city gates, insisting they leave this place and go to a place high in the mountains.

Sodom was in a valley, and Lot's family would have to work hard and climb in order to get to a higher place. Instead of agreeing, Lot asked if he could take his family to another nearby city that wasn't quite as high, and the angels agreed.

Lot's wife listened as the angels gave one simple instruction: "Do not stop or look back at Sodom."

For a while, she put one foot in front of the other and followed her husband, Lot. But at one point in the journey, she stopped moving. We don't know if she was curious to see what God had done to Sodom or if she missed her life there, but we do know this:

She looked back.

And the moment that she did, her body froze, turning into a pillar of salt.

She would remain there, her face toward the low valley of Sodom instead of the high mountain of refuge the Lord had provided.

Sodom was completely destroyed, and there in the distance of its rubble stood the shape of a woman, her eyes staring into the pit that she loved more than the goodness of God.

—FROM GENESIS 19

He

God is always **just**, which means He is fair with punishment and generous with grace. Part of His justice is punishing us when He decides it is best. When God tells us not to do something, He isn't playing a game with us. He wants us to take His rules very seriously and to know that He will hold us responsible for our decisions. We always have the choice to obey Him, but sadly, many times we don't.

Me

We should always pray and ask God to help us be wise in our decisions. When we know what He has told us and we deliberately ignore Him, we are putting ourselves in a very dangerous position. Ask God to help you make wise choices and to always seek Him when you aren't sure what to do. He wants to strengthen us, to guide us, and to encourage us into a place where we are obedient and wise, but we need to ask Him to help us do this.

She

Lord, help _Faith_ to speak to You from her heart whenever she is making choices. Teach her to make You the first place she goes when she is torn between the things of the world and the things of heaven. Help her to be wise in knowing what situations she needs to walk away from without looking back, and give her the courage to follow through. Teach her wisdom deep within her heart so that she will never stray from it (Psalm 51:6).

__Tsadaq__ (tsah DAK) is the Hebrew word for "justice."
The memory verse for this story is Genesis 19:26—
"But his wife looked back and became a pillar of salt."

Steadfast Love

The Story of Rebekah

As Rebekah gathered water from the well near her home, she didn't see him watching her. But he had been walking for miles to find her.

As Abraham's most trusted servant, he had been sent out to find a wife for Abraham's son Isaac, and he prayed that God would reveal the right woman to bring back to Canaan. He had finally reached Nahor, Abraham's hometown, and he prayed for wisdom on what to do next.

"Lord, show Your steadfast love to Abraham today. If I am speaking to the woman who is supposed to be Isaac's wife, I will ask her for a drink of water, and she will offer me some from the jug on her shoulder. Then, she will offer to get more from the well in order to water the ten camels that are with me." He hadn't finished speaking to God when he saw her, and even from a distance he could see she was beautiful.

As she filled the jar and began walking home, he stopped in front of her and asked for a drink. Rebekah was anxious to serve him and immediately gave him as much water as he needed. He waited, his heart pounding as she gently spoke.

"And your camels, sir. Please let me fetch more water for them as well." Rebekah hurried to the well again, balancing the heavy jar as he marveled at what the Lord had done.

She was the one.

The servant reached into his bag and took from it a ring and two beautiful golden bracelets. He held them out to her, asking if he might stay the night with her family. Abraham wanted his son to marry someone from their very own family, from their very own town, and now his servant was standing in front of a stranger who was God's answer to that prayer.

As soon as she told him the name of her father, he was sure.

The Lord had led him here, and His steadfast love for Abraham would surely bless the rest of his journey.

Rebekah raced home with the bracelets on her arms, gasping for breath as she told her family of the man by the well.

When he arrived, he told them the story from the beginning, explaining that his master was a great and powerful man who had the favor of God. As he told them about the water and the way Rebekah spoke, they nodded and smiled. The Lord Himself had certainly ordered his steps, and now she would return with him to Canaan and become Isaac's wife.

The next morning, the servant wasted no time. "Please, send me home to my master." Rebekah's family wanted her to stay at home a few more days, but Abraham's servant was anxious to get home and tell his master everything.

Not even a day ago, Rebekah had simply gone to fill a jug of water from the well as she did every day. Now her family was sending her away with their blessings and love.

They called to her, explaining that the servant wanted her to leave immediately. "Will you go with this man?" they asked.

It was undeniable that God's steadfast
love had designed this moment, and she
spoke quickly, realizing she was being written
into a much grander love story than she could have ever imagined.

"I will go."

As those three words fell from her mouth, the camels were readied, and
her family prayed for her life on the other side of the desert. She and her
nursemaids climbed onto the camels' backs, following the stranger straight
into God's plan.

The steadfast love of the God would bring them safely to the edge of Canaan.
As the first of the stars appeared in the sky, Rebekah saw a man in the distance. "Who is that man?" she asked.

Abraham's servant smiled. "That is the man you will marry."

Her heart beat faster as her fingers reached for the veil on her head, covering her face so he wouldn't see her until they were married. She listened
as Isaac spoke with his father's servant, and she watched as Isaac's eyes
danced with joy over her.

Isaac took Rebekah as his wife, and they began to build their life together
in Canaan, praying that one day soon they would have a baby of their own.
Little did they know, they were one prayer away from two more bright stars
in the starry sky of God's steadfast love.

—FROM GENESIS 24

He

Providence refers to the way God directs all things toward a worthy purpose. It means that when things might seem to us like a "coincidence" or "chance," there is really no such thing. He always takes care of us, always looks out for our best, and is part of our everyday lives. Not a single moment goes unseen by Him, and His plans for our lives have been in place since way before we were even born. He is such a good and kind Father to all of His children!

Me

If we choose to be kind to the people around us, they will notice. More than that, they will want to know the God who has led us to act this way. When someone does something hurtful or frustrates you, it's easy to want to yell and scream in return. But what does that show that person about God? It's much better to work hard at being kind in the same way your Father God has been kind to you.

She

Jesus, bless _Faith_ with the desire and ability to be kind to those You put in her path. Remind her what You have done for her and the way You have cared for the details of her life. Make it her joy to share that with the world through her joyful spirit. Fill her with Your love, Your passion for souls, and Your vision for the church, and allow her to be a witness to Your lovingkindness every single day of her life.

Checed (KHEH sed) is the Hebrew word for "lovingkindness."
The memory verse for this story is Genesis 24:40—
"The Lord before whom I have walked will send His angel with you
and make your journey a success."

The Veil

The Story of Rebekah, Rachel, and Leah

*A*fter struggling for years to get pregnant, Isaac prayed over his barren wife, Rebekah. Soon, she found out she was expecting twins!

As her belly grew round and full of life, Rebekah sensed something different about her babies. They seemed to be fighting all the time within her, and she asked the Lord why it was so. He explained that each of the two boys would grow to be the head of a nation, that they would never be at peace with one another, and that the older child would serve the younger.

When it came time for them to be born, Esau was delivered first. His body was covered with red, fuzzy hair. As he was almost out of Rebekah's womb, they noticed something very interesting about the second baby.

His hand was gripping Esau's heel, evidently trying to pull him back in. Even before Jacob was born, it seemed that he was fighting to take the rights of his firstborn brother.

One day, when they were older, Jacob stirred a delicious soup while Esau hungrily stared at it.

"Let me have some," Esau said.

"Okay," Jacob answered, "but first give me your birthright."

Esau was more concerned about his stomach than his legacy, so he agreed.

Esau had traded his rights as the firstborn for a bowl of soup. But there was one remaining blessing to be given to the firstborn. Rebekah wanted her favorite son, Jacob, to receive it instead of Esau, so she concocted a sneaky plan to deceive her very own husband.

Isaac was going blind, so Rebekah told Jacob to put the skins of young goats on his arms to make them feel hairy to Isaac's touch. Then, Rebekah cooked a meal to be passed off as Esau's offering to his father.

Years before she had offered water out of generosity and whispered words of obedience to God's plan. Now she offered a meal out of desperation, whispering words that God never told her to speak.

When the time was right, she sent Jacob into his father's room. At first, Isaac hesitated because he thought the voice was Jacob's. But feeling the hairy arms and smelling Esau's clothes convinced Isaac that this was indeed Esau. And again, a second-born son received the firstborn's blessing.

Jacob was fearful of what Esau might do to him when he found out, so he ran away from home and searched for a safe place to hide. Eventually he came to a town called Bethel where he hoped to find relatives that might help him. He went to a large well and asked the people nearby if they had heard of his uncle, Laban. They nodded and pointed to a woman walking toward them, explaining that she was Laban's daughter.

He couldn't believe what he was hearing; Rachel was exactly the woman he was supposed to marry, and he had found her. Jacob told Rachel who he was, kissing her as he cried tears of joy. The steadfast love of God had brought him to her, just as it had brought his mother to his father.

Laban heard that Jacob was there and ran from his house to meet him. He was overwhelmed with happiness and welcomed Jacob into his home, promising that he could marry Rachel after working for him for seven years.

Jacob loved Rachel so much that the years went by like hours, and finally their wedding day came. The bride wore a veil to cover her face just as his mother had done when she met his father. But this time, it wasn't because of tradition. It was because of treachery.

The dark night kept a secret that the morning sun would reveal: it wasn't Rachel under the veil, but her sister Leah instead. Jacob's father-in-law had tricked him, making him marry the older daughter instead of the younger one.

And so the one who tricked his own father was tricked by his father-in-law. Laban told Jacob he would give Rachel to him as well if he would agree to work for him for another seven years. Jacob again agreed.

Leah wasn't beautiful like Rachel, and she was never loved by Jacob the way Rachel was, so the Lord gave her the ability to have children while Rachel could not.

Leah gave her husband many sons in an effort to win his favor. But her hopes would be dashed every time another child was born, Jacob's eyes still looking past hers to Rachel's. When her fourth son was born, she finally looked to God instead of Jacob. She named the child "Judah" because it meant, "This time I will praise the Lord."

She had no idea that her praise was offered to the same Lord who would, many years later, come to earth as a baby from the same family of Judah.

As she rocked her son into the midnight hours, she may have wondered if she would ever be chosen.

But as sure as the stars lit the sky, God knew the answer.

You already have been, Love.

—FROM GENESIS 25–30

He

God doesn't feel love the way we do. In fact, the Bible says He is Love. It isn't an emotion that comes and goes for Him depending on our choices or our mistakes. There is nothing that can change the character of God, and that character is Love. We can be certain that God loves us because He tells us He does. That means that even in the moments when we feel like others don't care, or maybe like we have done something so terrible that God might stop loving us, we know the truth is that He can't. He won't. Not ever!

Me

Sometimes life doesn't seem fair at all to us. It's easy to look around and compare our lives to other people's and to think that maybe it's not right for them to have a nicer house or more things to play with. We might even start to be angry inside because we're wondering why life seems so unfair. Remember in these moments that you don't see everything the way that God does, and He chooses what He knows is best for you. That will look different from what He thinks is best for someone else. Even when it seems as if you didn't get what you wanted, think about the way He loves you. Just like Leah, He wants you to rely more on Him than anyone else around.

She

Lord, when life seems unfair to ___Faith___ and she's confronted with what she sees as injustice, overwhelm her with the truth of Your love and help her to follow the path of justice (Deuteronomy 16:20). Instead of stewing in her perceived lack, let her rejoice in the gain that is You. Help me to be a model to her of what godly reliance looks like, and the freedom that comes from admitting that I cannot see things the way You do. In her times of brokenheartedness, let her sense Your compassion and Your nearness, refusing to give in to a spirit of bitterness.

Yadah (yah DAH) is the Hebrew word for "praise."
The memory verse for this story is Genesis 29:35—
"This time I will praise the LORD."

The Women and the Water

The Story of Women in the Life of Moses

"The baby is coming," the midwife whispered, knowing that her loyalty to Pharaoh would be tested as soon as the child was born.

Pharaoh was the ruler of Egypt, and he had noticed how many Hebrew babies were being born there. He knew that those baby boys would grow to be strong men one day, and they just might become stronger than the Egyptians. He couldn't stand the thought, so he sent out a command to all the midwives who helped deliver Hebrew babies.

If the baby was a girl, she would be allowed to live. But the boys must be thrown in the Nile River to die, never to rise up against his people.

Jochebed knew what was at stake, and as she delivered her child, her heart was heavy for what might happen.

"It's a boy," the midwife said, her voice hushed.

Her loyalty to Pharaoh was nowhere near as strong as her loyalty to God, so she washed her hands, nodded kindly at the Hebrew family, and left the house without another word about the child.

The water should have swallowed him that day, but it didn't.

For months Jochebed hid her son, keeping him inside and quieting him when he cried, out of fear that they might be caught. When he was three months old, it was clear that they wouldn't be able to keep the secret much longer, and Jochebed did what she had to do to keep her family safe.

She went to the riverbank, and tears soaked her dress as she wove papyrus reeds together, forming a little basket that was just the right size for a sweet, little baby.

She took her son and laid him in it, covering him up with leaves and prayer.

With one last kiss, she pushed the basket into the river, watching as he drifted farther and farther from her.

Meanwhile, her daughter Miriam raced into the tall reeds of the water to follow the basket that held her baby brother. She wanted to see where it would go and what would become of him.

Pharaoh's daughter was bathing nearby, and she happened to see the basket floating in the distance. Miriam watched as Pharaoh's daughter called out to her maidservant and asked her to retrieve the basket. She removed the covering and realized it was a baby. Immediately she knew he must have been born to a Hebrew woman, and she took pity on the sweet child as he cried.

Seeing this as her chance, Miriam stepped out from the reeds and spoke to Pharaoh's daughter.

"If you would like, I can try to find a Hebrew woman to nurse him, and she will return him to you once he has grown a bit," she offered, hoping it would work.

Pharaoh's daughter agreed, and Miriam brought her brother back home to be cared for by his very own mother.

After he was old enough, he was returned to Pharaoh's daughter so she could raise him as her own son. She named him Moses, because it sounded like the word that meant "draw out," and she had drawn him out of the river and saved him.

The water should have swallowed him that day, but it didn't.

God had a plan for Moses that would lead him to become one of the greatest men in the history of Israel. He would grow to be a strong and courageous man who God handpicked to lead the Israelites out of Egypt and away from the abusive Pharaoh who had mistreated them for years.

When the time finally came for them to make their escape, thousands of Israelites were gathered and ready to flee with Moses as their leader. They were afraid, seeing no way to cross the sea which stood in the way of their freedom, but Moses reassured them.

"The Lord Himself is fighting for us," he told them. "Be still, and watch as He brings us forward safely."

But there was no way to swim that far, and the Egyptians were gaining ground as they chased after them. It looked to be an impossible situation, and many of the people cried out, wishing they had stayed in Egypt instead of facing certain death.

And then, the Lord spoke to Moses, commanding him to lift his staff in the air and stretch his hand out over the sea. He did, and immediately the waters miraculously split in half. Dry land spread out before them right in between the two walls of water.

Moses led the people, God's people, safely to the other side. But when the Egyptians tried to walk on the same dry path, the waters raged and trapped them instead. Not one survived the mighty waves, and Moses and the Israelites watched as the Egyptians were taken over by the sea.

The water should have swallowed him that day, but it didn't.

One midwife chose to keep him away from it.

One mother built a basket to keep him above it.

One sister watched as he traveled in it.

One daughter had lifted him out of it.

And all the while the one true God had watched, knowing that when it was time, He Himself would be the One to finally lead Moses and His people through it.

–from Exodus 1–2; 14

He

God is **majestic**, meaning that He is noble and excellent and worthy of all our praise. His name is far above all other names. His majesty tells us of His great splendor and power.

Me

One of the most important things we can strive to be as Christians is **faithful**. That means that we are constantly thinking about and acting on the things we know are best in the eyes of God. Being faithful isn't just a good choice we make once or twice, but a pattern of obedience that builds up over time and becomes our natural response. Even if it means we have to be brave in a scary time, or that we have to do something that feels like it wouldn't be the most fun or popular choice, we have to learn to be faithful followers of God. Whenever you feel let down or disappointed, or even afraid or unsure, think about this question: what would God want me to do in this moment? Eventually, you will start to do it without having to think as hard because you will be building up your spiritual muscles and honoring Him more and more as the days go by. It isn't easy, but it's right.

She

Lord, give ___Faith___ Your heart for the world, for Your people, and for Your Word. Let it truly become a lamp unto her feet and a light for her path (Psalm 119:105) as she finds herself in difficult situations. Remind her of the importance of faithful choices, even when they seem small. Let her grow to see the world as an opportunity to share Your goodness, and make her love for You the truest joy she knows. How majestic is Your name, Lord (Psalm 8:9)!

Howd *(HODE uh) is the Hebrew word for "majestic."*
The memory verse for this story is Exodus 3:14—
"God replied to Moses, 'I AM WHO I AM.'"

The Scarlet Cord

The Story of Rahab

Her house, built into a wall surrounding Jericho, gave her a magnificent view of everything that was hustling and bustling in the city.

Unfortunately, there wasn't much that was good for her eyes to see. The whole place had become infested with sin, and truth be told, she was a part of it. Rahab made her living by lying and sinning, and she was very good at being sneaky.

The Israelites had been wandering in the desert for forty years after escaping Egypt with Moses. They had been quick to forget how good God had been to them and spent much of their time complaining instead of being grateful. Because of that, God didn't let them walk directly to the land He had promised them. He knew that they weren't ready to be there.

But now the Israelites were near the entrance of Jericho again, and Joshua, the leader who had taken over when Moses died, was now determined to claim the land for the Israelites to call home. He and Caleb were the only two people who had told Moses they believed they could conquer it the first time, forty years earlier. But the people were afraid, and their doubt kept them from ever going in. They had died, and a new generation of people was ready to try again, this time without doubting God's power and promises.

The wall that protected the city would be their best chance at spying on things and making a plan to attack, so they decided to start there.

While Rahab was plotting all of the evil things she would do that day, God knew something that even she wouldn't have believed:

He was going to use her for good instead.

After hours of traveling, when the sun finally started to go down on the day, the two spies Joshua had sent out snuck their way into the city. They knew that they would have to hide quickly before anyone spotted them.

They found a door, which led to a house, which led to the woman God had chosen.

"Please," they begged her, "help keep us safe."

Rahab knew they were Israelites, and she knew that if she hid them in her house, she would be risking her life. The people in her city hated them and wanted them dead. If she turned them in instead, she would surely receive a wonderful reward.

But that night, the spies in her home and the sound of soldiers pounding on her door forced her to make a decision. She could choose to turn them in and continue her selfish life, or she could risk it all for a God she had only heard about.

Somehow, some way, she realized something in that moment that she hadn't known in her entire life.

She needed to be rescued, and they knew the Rescuer.

Quick as a flash, she hid the men on the roof. They could lie under the stalks of flax there and be completely unseen. She rushed to the front door, opening it wide to let God work through her obedience.

"What do you need?" she asked the soldiers at her door.

"Bring out the spies!" they shouted. "NOW!"

Rahab shook her head.

"They aren't here anymore," she began. "They were, but I didn't know they were spies. If you want to catch them, you'll have to run that way," she continued, her finger pointing to the city gate. "If you hurry, you'll get to them before the gate closes."

They believed her and ran into the night with their fists shaking and their swords drawn.

She lowered her finger, still trembling, and climbed up to the roof where the spies were hiding.

"I don't know your God," she whispered to them, "but I have heard of the things He has done, and I want to be on His side. I kept you safe, and now I want you to promise me that you'll do the same for me."

They agreed.

They told her that when they came back with all of their people, they would make sure Rahab and her family stayed safe. If she hung a long scarlet-red cord from her window, the Israelites would know that it was her house, and they would pass by it instead of attacking her.

When the walls of Jericho came crashing down, her house would remain.

A hand raised to lead the wicked into confusion would defend those who fight for God.

A finger pointing to a gate in the distance would ultimately point to her Redeemer Himself.

"The Lord your God, He is God in the heavens above," she had declared to the men that night. Little did she know that one sentence, spilled into the night like a scarlet cord, would make her His forever.

God had chosen a woman covered with shame to be His, and He would do it many, many more times.

—from Joshua 2

He

God loves **redemption**. The Bible is full of stories where people seemed terribly bad but God used them for good; His Word is full of the ugly things He made beautiful. When we read about men and women who made such awful choices and felt true hatred in their hearts, we can't help but wonder if God could ever make their stories wonderful again. The answer, of course, is that He can.

Me

We are never too "bad" for God to make "good." In fact, God loves to take the broken and ignored parts of life and breathe beauty into them, so there can be no question that it was His work. God calls us to be righteous, which means that we learn to see right and wrong by making God's Word the foundation of all our thinking and that we act from that understanding.

She

Lord, no matter how many mistakes _____ makes, show her the power of Your amazing grace. Lead her to stories in Scripture where she can see the transformation that comes from a life hidden in Christ. When she stumbles and she sins, help her to stand back up in repentance and move forward without a sense of condemnation. Let every day be a day where she wakes up, remembers Your new mercy, and purposes to walk every step before her out of a true desire to honor You as You give her grace upon grace (John 1:16).

Amats (aw MATS) is the Hebrew word for "courageous."
The memory verse for this story is Joshua 2:18—
"When we enter the land, you tie this scarlet cord to the window
through which you let us down."

Covering

The Story of Deborah and Jael

The Israelites had finally made it into the land God had promised them, but instead of remembering His goodness, they began to live as if they had forgotten Him completely.

They had heard stories of God's faithfulness since they were little children. Their parents and grandparents whispered about the sea splitting in two and told of the bread that fell from heaven so they would always have food.

And yet, they turned away from Him over and over again.

The Israelites wanted to serve other gods and live by their own rules, but every time they tried, things would go terribly wrong. God would stop protecting them, and He would allow their enemies to beat them in battle. Eventually they would become so desperate that they would cry out to God for relief. Because He loved them so much, He would send a person called a judge to help.

The judge would lead the people into victory over their enemies and remind them of God's laws, urging them to obey Him and live in His favor. It would work for a while, but eventually they would go back to their own ways. And the pattern would continue.

Under the swaying leaves of a palm tree, a wise woman sat and shared God's truth with people who had traveled from miles around to listen to her. They knew she believed in God wholeheartedly and that she heard His voice in a way they didn't.

Her name was Deborah, and she was chosen by God to be a judge over the Israelites after they had been defeated by the Canaanites. She would sit still as the wind blew, listening for the voice of God to give her instructions. One day, she knew that He was telling her to call for a commander named Barak and inform him that it was time to go to war with the Canaanites.

Barak hesitated. "I'll only go if you'll go with me," he told Deborah.

The leader of the Canaanites was a ruthless man named Sisera, and his army was much more powerful than Barak's. To Barak, it looked like certain death.

But as children of God, we don't walk where we see the easiest battle or the weakest army; we walk where God tells us to walk. Deborah knew that God was calling them into this battle, and she trusted Him to secure their victory one way or another.

"I'll go with you," she told Barak, "but you won't get credit for winning the war. A woman will be responsible for Sisera's death." Barak's little faith would receive little reward.

As they got closer to the Canaanites, the Israelites walked through wet, marshy land with ease. They didn't have a lot of weapons and armor to weigh them down, but the Canaanites did. Sisera had brought hundreds of chariots to ensure his victory, but the wheels became trapped in the mud, and the horses frantically kicked their legs to escape the sinking ground. The very thing that made the Israelites seem weak in battle is what gave them the upper hand, their legs steady while the chariots spun into chaos.

Sisera ran from the battle to save himself, and when he got far enough away to consider himself safe, he found a woman to help him. Her name was Jael, and she welcomed him into her tent with kindness and generosity, reassuring him that he didn't need to be afraid.

He lay down on the ground, and she covered him gently with a rug to keep him warm. When he asked for a drink of water, she brought him milk instead. As he drank it, he became sleepy and let his eyes close. Quietly, she went outside the tent and pulled up one of the pegs that secured it to the ground. With the tent peg in one hand and a hammer in the other, she snuck back into the tent and pounded the peg right into Sisera's head while he was sleeping.

Jael had killed the wicked leader, and just as Deborah had predicted, Barak lost the opportunity to be seen as a hero because he had doubted the power of God.

Deborah's voice pierced the darkness in a song of victory, praising the God who had been merciful with them yet again.

The palm tree was really God covering Deborah while she spoke His words.

The marshland was really God covering the ground to trap the enemies of His people.

The rug was really God covering Sisera in order for His will to be done.

And the night sky, flecked with radiant stars, was really God covering His people so that one day they would realize that's exactly what they were: *His*.

—FROM JUDGES 4

He

God is **dependable**—His ultimate plan always prevails. When someone doesn't step up and do her job, it doesn't cancel God's intentions. Things happen in the world, and it's easy to wonder if God meant for them to happen. How could a God who loves us so much allow horrible things? The truth is that Satan is a powerful enemy, and he has come to steal, kill, and destroy (John 10:10). He will do his best to do that, and sometimes God will allow Satan to get his way. But even that, as awful as it seems in the moment, will not change the plan God has for good. God does not take pleasure in our pain, and He comforts those with heavy hearts and teary eyes.

Me

Are you dependable? Do people know that even if it's hard, you will keep your word and do the things you have said you are going to do? There are so many situations in the Bible where we see people come up against what seem like impossible odds, but they go on to do what God has asked them to do instead of backing down. It's important to be a person on whom other people can depend and trust.

She

Jesus, help _____ to remember that nothing You have asked her to do or will ask her to do is outside the scope of Your power and the length of Your arm (Isaiah 59:1). Create in her a desire to hear Your voice and to be a dependable servant of everything You have entrusted to her. When the world seems to rise against her and indicate certain failure, remind her that You love to take the weak and show Your strength through them. Teach her the value of living a life that leans hard into You and chooses the good, hard things that You have asked of her. In my life, let me be someone who demonstrates the courage and faithfulness that honor You and the strength that comes from relying more on You than what my hands can touch.

Shaphat (shah FOT) is the Hebrew word for "judge."
The memory verse for this story is Judges 4:14—
"Hasn't the Lord gone before you?"

Pieces of Silver

The Story of Delilah

"He's in love with you, Delilah," the lords explained to her. "He will tell you his secrets, and when you tell them to us, we will pay you."

She listened to the Philistines, thinking about the man they were referring to. His name was Samson, and he was one of the judges of Israel. His strength was legendary, but nobody knew where it came from. If the Philistines found out, they would be able to conquer him.

Even as a boy Samson had possessed incredible power, once killing a lion with his bare hands. But for such a strong man, he certainly had his weaknesses as well.

"Each of us will give you 1,100 pieces of silver if you are able to help us," the men promised Delilah.

That was 5,500 pieces of silver altogether, and even though it meant betraying Samson, Delilah had her weaknesses too. She nodded at the men, waved them away, and plotted against the man who loved her.

"Samson," Delilah whispered sweet as honey, "what would take away your power and allow someone to capture you?"

Two other women had tricked him in the past, and he wasn't sure if he should trust her.

"Well," he began, "if I were to be tied down with seven fresh bowstrings, I would be helpless."

The lords brought her the bowstrings, and she tied him with them while he slept, but as soon as he awoke, he broke right through them.

"You lied to me!" Delilah shouted. "I want to know the truth."

He told her that new ropes used against him would make him powerless, but after she tied him up again, he woke up and ripped them away with hardly any effort.

"Again you have lied to me. You have made a fool of me!" Still Delilah asked him again, and this time he told her that if she wove together the seven locks of his hair, he would be powerless. She waited until he was asleep and twisted his hair gently, pinning it tightly.

"The Philistines are here!" she screamed to see if he could fight.

He ripped out the pin and untangled his hair, knowing she had tried to trick him again. But Samson's strength was in his arms, not his will, and he could not bring himself to leave beautiful Delilah.

Delilah could see that Samson wasn't going to tell her the truth, and she wanted to be rich more than she wanted to be good, so she forced hot tears down her cheeks as she begged him once again.

"You must not really love me," she cried, "because you don't trust me enough to tell me the truth." Day after day she pressed those words into his heart until at last he couldn't bear to keep it from her anymore.

"My hair," he said, his eyes staring into hers. "I am a Nazarite, a man who serves God, and I have never, ever cut my hair."

Indeed it was true. Before Samson was even born, an angel had come to his parents to tell them that they would have a son who would be a Nazarite. In order to fulfill his duties, there were certain things he couldn't do, and one of them was to cut his hair. His parents honored the words of the Lord, and a razor had never touched his head.

If it did, his strength would leave him.

Delilah sensed that Samson was sharing all of his heart with her, and she listened as he finally trusted her with his life.

As soon as she could, she called to the lords and told them to be ready.

When she saw the opportunity, she smiled lovingly at him, wooing him to rest his head on her knees. As his eyes closed, her fingers smoothed his golden hair, but her thoughts were of silver.

The men cut his hair quietly while he rested, and as the last of the seven locks fell to the ground, Delilah shouted for the last time, "Samson, wake up! You're being attacked by the Philistines!"

He tried to kick and punch, but it was of no use. He realized that the Lord had taken his power, and there was nothing he could do to defend himself. The Philistines tortured Samson, poking out his eyes and binding his hands with shackles.

His weakness for Delilah had cost him his strength.

One day, Samson was called out to entertain thousands who had gathered so they could laugh at his weakness. But while he had been imprisoned by the Philistines, his hair had begun to grow back again.

As blind Samson stood in front of thousands of people, he asked a young man to help him find the pillars of the house so he could lean against them. He put his right hand on one and his left hand on the other, and he prayed that God would give him one more moment of strength before he died.

God granted his request. As Samson pushed the pillars apart, the entire house fell and killed everyone there, including him.

But what about Delilah? What became of her?

We don't know, because her name is never mentioned in the Bible again. What we do know is that when her name is spoken, even to this day, it is fastened like a pin, woven in a web, and bound like a fresh rope to his.

For all she did to bring him ruin, she will forevermore be known as a woman of deceit, the one who took his whole heart and traded it for pieces of silver.

—FROM JUDGES 16

He

God is **truth**. He cannot lie, and there is nothing in Him that is fake or false or sneaky. His enemy, Satan, is the father of lies, and you can be sure that he wants you to listen to the wicked way he is spinning the truth of God. God's promises are true, His goodness is true, and His love for you is true. All of the things that He tells us in Scripture are true, and we can put our full trust in Him, knowing that He has not, cannot, and will never tell a lie.

Me

God wants us to be like Him, and one of the ways we can do this is to be honest. We should never be two-faced, telling people lies in order to manipulate our lives. There are times in the Bible when people lie and God blesses them in spite of it, but we should never think that it was the only way He could have used them. In other words, there is never a time when lying is the only choice we have. God wants us to be honest. When we trick the people around us or use their trust in us to betray them, we disappoint God.

She

Lord, let Your Word be a constant reminder and inspiration for _____. When she is in a position where she has to choose between integrity and what she perceives as success, remind her of the way You despise dishonesty and desire Your daughters to speak words of truth. Give her the courage to stand her ground, even when it's hard, refusing to compromise her honesty for the sake of a temporary benefit. Let the words of her mouth and the meditation of her heart be pleasing in Your sight, Lord (Psalm 19).

*'**Emeth** (EH met) is the Hebrew word for "truth."*
The memory verse for this story is Judges 16:28—
"Lord GOD, please remember me. Strengthen me, God, just once more."

Redeemer

The Story of Naomi and Ruth

"I will miss you terribly," Naomi whispered, hugging the two women her sons had married. She loved them as if they were her own. But now that Naomi's sons—their husbands—had died, the women were no longer bound to stay with her.

Naomi was leaving Moab for Bethlehem, and the women would naturally stay in their own land. Naomi's husband had died as well, and she thought it would be best to return to her hometown where extended family might be able to care for her now that she was alone.

Orpah and Ruth told Naomi that they would go with her, but she shook her head.

"Moab is your home. Stay here, and God will surely redeem your losses by bringing husbands for each of you." She wiped her cheeks, hot with tears, trying to reassure them that she would be all right.

She had been a foreigner in their land for years, and she knew how difficult it was. She didn't want to uproot them and cause them the same heartache she had suffered.

And yet, they walked with her.

After they had traveled some distance, she stopped again, pointing back to Moab.

"Go back, girls." Her voice was stern. "You have been so good to me, and I pray your kindness is repaid, but this is not the way." She stood her ground, insisting this was the end of their time together.

At last, Orpah obeyed her and turned back, weeping as she ran away from them.

Then Naomi's eyes met Ruth's. "Go, child. Follow her back."

But Ruth refused to leave her. Her mind was made up, and her feet would follow Naomi's to Bethlehem.

"Where you go, I go," Ruth began, her voice steady with determination. "Your home is my home now, and your God is my God." The cord of loyalty that bound Ruth's heart to her mother-in-law would not be severed by anything but death.

Naomi listened, her heart warmed by the unwavering devotion of a woman who owed her nothing.

When the two women had settled in Bethlehem, Ruth found a relative of Naomi's deceased husband and decided she would go to his field to gather food. It was common for the needy to take leftover grain from the edges of a field, picking up whatever might be left when the farmers finished their work. From a distance, Boaz, the owner of the field, saw Ruth and asked one of his workers who she was.

"She is the Moabite woman who returned with Naomi. She stays here from early morning until evening and hardly takes a break," he explained.

Boaz had heard of Ruth and went to her as she worked. He assured her that she was welcome there. Not only that, but he told her that she need not work anywhere else. When he offered her water and kindness, she fell to the ground in gratitude.

"Why me?" she whispered, not even daring to look him in the eye. "This land isn't mine, and you owe me nothing. I'm not yours to care for." Her voice shook as she considered the gift he offered—a gift she didn't deserve.

"You have made a choice that honors God by leaving everything you know in order to care for Naomi. I pray that He redeems your sacrifice fully. This is the least I can do to honor you." His gentleness left her speechless.

She returned home to Naomi that evening, her face flushed and her arms full with food. When Naomi asked her where it had come from, Ruth explained what had happened. As Naomi listened, one word echoed louder than the rest, and a smile crept across her face.

Boaz.

Naomi knew something about him that could change everything.

"Ruth," she interrupted, hushing her with excitement, "Boaz is your redeemer."

Immediately, Ruth understood. Based on his position in the family, the very man who had offered her grain could offer her marriage as well.

"Go to him while he's sleeping," Naomi said to her. "Lie at the foot of his bed and lift the covers off of his feet. When he sees you there, he will understand."

Ruth nodded, hardly believing all that had happened. She did exactly as her mother-in-law had said. As Boaz awoke, he asked who was there.

"It is me, Ruth," she said quietly. "I am yours if you will have me as your wife."

The moonlight snuck in through the walls as she waited for his response.

Boaz told her he would marry her gladly, and he made all the arrangements to do so. He was a man of honor—that was certain.

But none of this would have happened if it hadn't been for Boaz's own mother.

Because one night, before he had even been born, she had hidden spies under stalks of flax on her rooftop before a scarlet cord saved her. She had decided many of the same things Ruth had, her heart bound to what was right and good before God.

Your God will be my God.

I will leave everything I know in order to follow you.

And when the harvest is ripe, even though you owe me nothing, you will give me a gift that I don't deserve and can never repay.

Many years later, with four words, one of Boaz and Ruth's great-great-great grandchildren would do just that and change the world forever.

I am your Redeemer. . . .

—FROM THE BOOK OF RUTH

He

The Lord is our **Provider**, and He delights in being our security. He sees our hearts, understands our struggles, and hears all the prayers we offer Him. He knows when we are worried about the future and when it seems like we don't have enough. But He knows—and He wants you to know—that He is not limited by our circumstances. He is our true Provider, the One who wants us to have all the good gifts that come from trusting Him to be exactly that.

Me

Think about the times in your life when you have been loyal, when you have stuck by someone's side instead of walking away, when you cared about her situation as well as your own. When we choose to be loyal, we are showing others the way Jesus loves them and will never leave them. When you have the chance to stand by the people you love, even if it's hard or uncomfortable, God honors Your decisions.

She

Lord, create in _____ a strong sense of empathy and devotion, where she develops a longing for solidarity and secure relationships that reflect You. When she has opportunities to show herself as a loyal friend, bring to her mind the way that You love and reward our choices to be trustworthy companions, even when it comes at a cost to us. Give her people who will do the same for her—friends she can count on to be loyal and true. When she experiences the consequences of disloyalty, instead of becoming bitter or hurt, allow her to be reminded of the blessing we are to others when we show them that we are worthy of their trust (Proverbs 17:17).

Ga-al (gah AHL) is the Hebrew word for "redeemer."
The memory verse for this story is Ruth 1:16—
"Your people will be my people, and your God will be my God."

The Needle

The Story of Hannah

$\mathcal{H}$annah watched her feet as they moved one in front of the other, trying to think of something other than the words being thrown at her.

"You have nothing to give him, Hannah. You can't have children, and you'll always be second-best because of it." Peninnah laughed as her own children ran up ahead of them. "You're useless to Elkanah."

Hannah knew that Elkanah loved her, but Peninnah was right. She hadn't been able to have children with him, and it devastated her.

She turned her focus back to the task at hand and prayed as they continued walking. Every year they made this same journey to Shiloh to give the Lord an offering. It was a chance to show their devotion to God, even though most of the people around them had long given up on serving Him.

But not Elkanah. He was a man who believed in God and wanted his life to show it. God's rules were important to him, and he made it a priority to respect them. Prayer covered their lives. Every moment given to them was one received in gratitude and recognition of the Giver.

Peninnah, unkind as she was, would never affect the way Hannah trusted God.

When they got to the temple to give their offerings, Hannah took a few moments to kneel and pray. Her sadness overwhelmed her, and her eyes filled with tears.

"If You give me a son," she prayed, "I will give him back to You, and he will serve You for his entire life. I promise, Lord." As the words passed through her mind, she sighed, desperate for hope.

From across the room, the high priest, Eli, had been watching her. He hadn't heard a sound come from her, but he watched her mouth moving and assumed she had been drinking too much wine. Things were so bad at that time, it was easier to believe that she was filled with wine than faith.

He went to her, rebuking her for such a sinful decision, but her eyes returned his accusations with truth.

"My lord," Hannah whispered to him, "I have had nothing to drink—nothing at all. I am only here weeping before the Lord and pouring my heart out to Him." He studied her red eyes, realizing she was a woman who was suffering in her sorrow.

Eli could see she was desperate, and instead of giving her words that scratched her heart, like Peninnah did, he gave her words that soothed her soul.

"May God give you what you have asked Him for," Eli replied kindly, praying for peace as she traveled home.

His words fed her hope, and she found herself smiling instead of crying.

The Lord did answer her prayer, giving her a baby boy whom she named Samuel. And true to her word, as soon as he was old enough, she brought him to the temple in Shiloh where she had met Eli years before.

Seeing Eli, she walked over to him with her son and reminded Eli who she was. Of course, he didn't know that she had made a promise to God, but he listened as she explained.

"God gave me the son I prayed for, and I got to hold him in my arms for a little while," she said. "But I gave Him my word, and today I am here to keep my promise."

Hannah's arms had held Samuel, but he belonged to the Lord.

Samuel would live there at the temple, serving God day and night alongside Eli. It blessed Eli to have Samuel's company because neither of his sons cared about God at all.

Every year, Hannah sewed her son a special coat to wear and brought it to the temple for him. God blessed her with more children, and as always, she thanked Him for His kindness to her.

It would be easy to think this was a sad ending for Hannah because she didn't get to take care of Samuel, but it wasn't—not for her. As her fingers worked day after day on his coats, she would smile, knowing she was making them not just for Samuel, but for the Lord Himself.

After all, Samuel would grow to be one of the finest men in the nation, seeking God above everything else. He lived his days sharing truth and building God's kingdom, just as his mother had prayed he would.

Hannah lived her life in prayer and praise, holding the promises of God as tightly as her sewing needle, knowing all along that He was worthy of the honor.

–from 1 Samuel 1–3

He

God is the only true source of **peace** we will ever really know. Only He is able to give us a "peace that passes understanding" (Philippians 4:7) and a sure sense that He is with us and for us at all times. In the busy and trouble-filled world, it's important that we remember that we have this anchor for our souls and that He offers us the gift of His peace no matter what is happening around us.

Me

When it seems like things aren't happening the way we want them to, we can be sure that God is asking us to be patient and wait for Him. There will be times when we have asked Him for things over and over again, and we will be tempted to believe He doesn't care or that He isn't listening. Neither of those is true, of course. Instead of thinking the worst of God, try seeing it as an opportunity to practice your patience. He will come through!

She

Jesus, make _____ a girl who reaches to You first when she is in bumpy times. Give her the peace that only You can give, so that she learns what it is like to wait for You, to call out to You, and to eventually take on Your peace instead of the worry of the world. Let her heart be so wedded to Yours that in the instant she feels threatened or afraid, she will call Your name (2 Samuel 22:4). Bless her with Your undeniable presence and the assurance of Your care for her until she can't imagine looking anywhere else for security.

Shalowm (shah LOWM) is the Hebrew word for "peace."
The memory verse for this story is 1 Samuel 2:2—
"There is no one holy like the LORD. There is no one besides You!
And there is no rock like our God."

Swords and Stones

The Story of Abigail

It didn't surprise Abigail that her husband, Nabal, had let his temper get the best of him again, but this time the consequences were disastrous. David and his men were now headed straight for Abigail's house, and the men weren't going to leave until Nabal's entire family was dead.

David was on the run from King Saul, who had become a madman. For a while, Saul had adored David because his soothing harp brought peace when nothing else would. But when King Saul realized that people were beginning to love David more than him, the king's jealousy turned love into hatred, and he became determined to murder David.

While David was hiding from King Saul, he was asking for help from anyone he could. He remembered a wealthy man named Nabal whom he had protected in the past, so David sent a request to him for food. Instead of returning the favor, Nabal ridiculed David and refused to give him a single meal.

David was furious, and now he was out for revenge. All of their lives were at stake, but Nabal was too stubborn to care.

Of course, Nabal had heard the stories of David. Everyone had. David had been chosen by God when he was just a boy shepherding his father's flocks, and one day he would be their king. Whenever his name came up in conversation, so did the story of the stone.

"One stone," they would whisper in awe. "All the strongest men in the army were too scared to fight against the great giant, but David defeated Goliath with just one stone."

David was a legend, a hero, and their future leader. But none of that mattered to Nabal—he couldn't see past his own pride.

Abigail knew she had to do something, and she quickly called to her servants. They loaded up several donkeys with bread and meat, raisins and fig cakes. If she could just get to David before David got to them, maybe she could make things right.

"Go on ahead," she called to the servants. "And when you get to him, tell him I am coming."

She hurried down the mountain, and when she reached the bottom, she could see David and his four hundred men in the distance. There, in the shadow of the great mountain, she climbed from her donkey and ran to him, falling at his feet.

"Please, my lord, let the blame for all of this be on me alone," she begged. "I didn't know you had asked for food, or I would have gladly given it to you, especially knowing what you have done for us in the past."

David listened.

"My husband has made a terrible mistake, but you are about to make a terrible mistake in return." She paused, praying her words would change his mind. She knew she was taking a chance, but she also knew that she was speaking truth.

"You will one day be king over all this land, and you don't want to look back and regret this. This is not a battle God has called you to fight, my lord. Let Him take care of Nabal instead," she finished, her eyes still focused on David's feet.

Her heart pounded as she waited for his response.

David considered all that she had said, and he knew she had protected him as much as she had protected her own husband. She was right; he didn't want the blood of Nabal on his sword, staining his legacy with a hasty decision. If he killed Nabal and his people, he would be no better than Saul.

"Praise God for sending you to me today," David said softly to the woman. "Your wisdom and kindness have saved us all from harm. Please, go home in peace."

He watched as she rose up from the ground and walked slowly to her donkey. Her knees were stained with the dirt of bowing in humility. As she faded into the heights of the mountain, her words continued to soothe him like a delicate harp.

When Abigail told Nabal what had happened, he went into shock and died ten days later. The Lord had taken revenge instead of David, and David's name was left untainted as a result of heeding Abigail's wise advice.

Once again David sent his men to the house of Nabal. This time, it was not to request a hand of help, but rather a hand of marriage.

And once again, Abigail bowed low to the ground in humility, accepting his offer.

She knew the truth all along, of course: swords and armies were no match for a man who sought the heart of God. She traveled back down the mountain, all the way to David, honored to hold the hand that had once thrown a small, smooth stone of faith into a battle he was called to fight.

—FROM 1 SAMUEL 25

He

The Lord is **wise** beyond measure, and He uses this wisdom to guide our steps and determine how we are best used for His kingdom. He has all the details we don't have, and He knows when it's best to give and when it's best to withhold. In His infinite wisdom, He invites us into a relationship with Him where we can know Him and listen as He leads us.

Me

Being prudent means that we wait for the right time to do the right thing. We don't act out of our own impatience, and we don't give in when our minds tell us we have to get our way. When we wait on the Lord, asking for His guidance and presence, we will know when it's time to act and when it's best to hold our opinions and our actions close instead.

She

Lord, give _____ a strong desire to act according to Your will, in ways that are well-watered with Your grace. Help her to hold her tongue when she wants to speak from her own hurts and to be someone who listens for Your voice and moves when You call her in exactly the way You call her. Let her learn the art of waiting (Ecclesiastes 7:8) and of discerning when You are urging her to go forward. When she has done this, bring her the peace that comes from living alongside such a good God and the security that belongs to those who rely on Your wisdom before our own.

*'**Arek** (aw RAKE) is the Hebrew word for "patient."*
The memory verse for this story is 1 Samuel 25:28 ESV—
"For the LORD will certainly make my lord a sure house, because my lord
is fighting the battles of the LORD."

Clean

The Story of Bathsheba

One warm spring evening, Bathsheba went outside to bathe.

That in itself wasn't uncommon, but what happened next certainly was.

King David had been resting in his palace even though he should have been fighting in a war. As the sun began to set, he walked out on the roof to get some fresh air. As he walked, he caught a glimpse of the beautiful Bathsheba.

He asked his servants who she was, and when they told him her name, he knew right away that she was married. In fact, her husband Uriah was one of his mightiest warriors, and he was on the battlefield at that very moment.

David sent for Bathsheba, ignoring anything in his conscience that told him it was wrong, and she came to the palace to be with him.

Some time later, a message arrived at the palace, and King David's blood ran cold.

It was from Bathsheba, and it simply said that she was going to have a baby. He knew that he was the baby's father, and he panicked. He tried to trick Uriah into thinking he was the father, but it didn't work.

So David made one of the worst decisions of his life, sending a command to one of his officers.

"Put Uriah on the front lines," he ordered. It would be certain death for Uriah, but it was the only way David could imagine to keep his sin hidden.

Poor Uriah. He was a good and godly man, and he died because David wanted to protect himself. But David was caught up in his pride and tangled in the love of a woman who wasn't his.

And Bathsheba, who probably had no idea that David was responsible, mourned the loss of her husband when she heard he had died.

After she'd had time to mourn, David sent for Bathsheba again. This time, he brought her to the palace to become his wife.

He watched as her stomach grew larger with their son, and the time finally came for the baby to be born. Bathsheba became a mother, but it wouldn't last long.

Nathan, a dear friend of David's, confronted David about what the Lord had revealed to him. He knew that David was guilty, and God had told him what David's punishment would be.

"The child will not survive much longer," Nathan told David.

When the baby became ill, David laid down on the floor of his grand estate and begged God to spare the child. David refused to eat food and spent a week in prayer for the boy Bathsheba had given him.

On the seventh day, the child died.

David rose up from the ground and stood tall, finally washing his clothes and leaving to go and worship the Lord. When he returned, his servants were confused and asked him why he seemed to be at peace. He told them that he knew that the child was now with God and that even though he couldn't raise him on this earth, he would see him again in heaven.

Bathsheba was devastated, and David comforted her as she cried.

Could their sin ever be forgiven?

God gave them their answer in the form of another baby, a baby that He had wonderful plans for. David and Bathsheba named him Solomon, and in the cry of fresh life, they were humbled at God's mercy.

Sin doesn't wash away in a spring bath, but rather, through the grace of a God who is patient with His children. Although David was forgiven, he was also punished for what he had done and was never able to build the grand temple for God that he had always wanted to build.

With the sketches piled up and the plans in place, he gave everything to his son, Solomon, who would be the builder instead of him.

Years earlier, Abigail had warned him not to kill her husband because she knew it would be a stain upon his life.

Fight the battles God has called you to fight, David. Leave the rest to Him.

—FROM 2 SAMUEL 11–12

He

God is **self-sufficient**, which means He doesn't need anything from us. In fact, He doesn't need us at all—He *chose* us. He wants us to want a relationship with Him. When people deny Him or turn their backs on Him, it doesn't change who He is at all; it only changes who they are.

Me

It's important to remember that the world is looking at us as examples of God. As we make decisions, we need to be constantly aware of this. It affects everything we do, even down to the kinds of clothes we wear! Our bodies are temples of God (1 Corinthians 6:19), and we should choose to clothe ourselves in a way that honors our heavenly Father. Be modest and aware of what your clothing tells people about you. Do you respect the temple that God has given you? If you do, you will cover it in ways that are honoring to God instead of looking to the rest of the world to tell you what's appropriate.

She

Lord, help _____ to remember that although You don't need her in order to be God, she needs You. Because we have been chosen, we need to remember that even our bodies aren't our own and that they belong to You. Give her such a strong foundation in You that she isn't bound by whatever the latest trends are. Create in her a pure heart (Psalm 24:4) and a desire to keep herself pure, even in the way she clothes herself. Allow her modesty to be a reflection of respect for You, speaking loudly to a watching world.

__Chemah__ (kay MAH) is the Hebrew word for "wrath."
The memory verse for this story is 2 Samuel 11:27—
*"However, the L*ORD *considered what David had done to be evil."*

Anything

The Story of the Queen of Sheba

Solomon had fallen asleep with a heavy heart, fully aware of the responsibility that now rested on his shoulders. His father, David, had given him not only full control of the kingdom, but also the task of building a grand temple for God.

For years Solomon had seen his father working on the elaborate drawings and gathering materials from around the world. Now, all of it was up to him. He was young and inexperienced, and he worried that he wouldn't honor his father. Worse than that, he was worried that he wouldn't honor God.

In his dreams that night, he heard the voice of God asking him a question. *Solomon, I will give you anything you want. . . . What will you ask for?*

Solomon answered with the first thing that came to mind. It wasn't money or even a long, healthy life, but rather that he would make good decisions and have the wisdom he needed to lead the nation well.

He could have chosen anything, and he chose to be wise.

This made God happy, and He knew that Solomon had a good heart and wanted to please Him. He not only made Solomon the smartest man in the world; He also gave him incredible wealth as well.

Pretty soon, people were traveling from all over to sit with Solomon and ask him questions, and they never failed to walk away amazed at his answers.

All the while, he put his heart and soul into building the temple, overseeing all the work and studying the details to make sure everything was just right. When the temple was complete, it stood high above the ground, covered in jewels, gold, and intricate carvings. The temple was supposed to be a building that represented God's presence so that the people would be able to look at it and think of the majesty of God. More than anything, Solomon wanted it to honor Him.

95

One day, a very rich and famous queen decided that she had to go and see all of this for herself. She could hardly believe that a man could be as wise as she had heard Solomon was, and she wanted to look at this amazing temple with her own eyes.

The queen of Sheba lived over a thousand miles from Solomon, but she didn't let that stop her from making the difficult journey. She packed up as many gifts as she could and began the trip with several of her servants. She wanted to know Solomon's secret, and if that meant weeks of travel, it was worth it.

When she finally arrived, she was captivated. The temple was so much grander than anything she imagined, even more beautiful than her wildest dreams. She sat with Solomon and asked him question after question, soaking up his answers in awe.

The queen longed for truth, and when Solomon spoke about his God, she heard it.

In her country, there were dozens of gods. So many, in fact, that it would be hard to count. Her people believed the gods all had different jobs and powers, so the people just prayed to all of them. As far as the one true God? They didn't know Him at all.

The queen was impressed by all the sparkling, shining things, but she had plenty of those herself. What amazed her the most was the way Solomon spoke about God and honored His name more than any other.

It was clear that Solomon's God loved him and blessed him, and she couldn't help but wonder if any of her gods could match His power.

When the time came for her to leave, she gave Solomon all the gifts she had brought, piling up spices and treasures in gratitude. And in return, Solomon offered her something as well. In fact, he offered her anything she wanted.

She accepted his offer by gathering up everything she could manage to carry home with her. But those were just things, and they wouldn't last forever. Perhaps one day the queen of Sheba would realize that the only thing more incredible than the gifts was the real Giver of the gifts: God Himself.

After all, she had traveled a long, long way to find truth.

And Solomon, the wisest man who ever lived, had certainly offered her that.

—from 1 Kings 3; 10

He

God is **knowledge**, and we can never get to the bottom of everything He knows. He's been here since before the world began, and He created everything in it. He knows the entire history of the world, the science of how everything works, and every tiny detail about every single person who has ever and will ever exist. God knows all of the secrets of heaven and earth—there simply is no end to His knowledge!

Me

Isn't it amazing that we can talk to the same God who put the stars in the sky? And that infinite knowledge is extended to us. No matter how much we search, there will always be more to know and understand, and the more we pray and seek it, the wiser we will become. Still, don't ever let yourself believe that you know enough to take on your own problems alone. Always be someone who is eager to learn, praying for opportunities to know more about God.

She

Jesus, inspire _____ to be a daughter who is always hungry to know more of You (Proverbs 2:4). Give her a zeal for searching out Your truth, and let her not grow weary as she seeks You. When she is around her friends, her teachers, her relatives, and any other people You put in her path, let her constantly be looking to see more of You in them. Give her mentors and lifelong friends who will teach her well, and maintain in her a genuine sense of wonder at who You are and the way You love her.

__Chokmah__ (kok MAH) is the Hebrew word for "wisdom."
The memory verse for this story is 2 Chronicles 9:8—
"May the L<small>ORD</small> your God be praised! He delighted in you and put you
on His throne as king for the L<small>ORD</small> your God."

Painting Her Face

The Story of Jezebel

$\mathcal{K}$ing Ahab knew that a Jew like himself should never take a bride who loved another god, but when he met Jezebel he decided that she was worth taking a chance. She was spectacularly beautiful, and she convinced him that she was the best choice for him.

All the while, the wickedness inside her grew. She hated God, and she wanted everyone in the land to hate Him too.

She slithered around the palace like a snake, demanding that Ahab do as she ordered. He was too weak-minded to stand up for what was right, so he let her boss him around. Using her husband's power, she would try to make everyone in Israel believe in Baal instead of God.

With lipstick in her hand, she colored her mouth blood-red and smiled at her reflection.

She knew that she could get him to do whatever she pleased, and it made her dizzy with happiness. If she had her way, the Israelites would be converted in no time, and God would be a distant memory.

Every day it went like this: she combed and braided and powdered and buttoned until she looked like a glamorous queen. It seemed to hide what was underneath.

One afternoon she heard her husband come into the house, and it was clear he was furious. She followed the sound of his voice into the bedroom, where she saw him lying down with his face toward the wall.

"Ahab, what is the matter?" she asked, always searching for a way to use him for her own schemes.

"I went to buy land that I wanted today, and the man refused to sell it to me," he answered. "Naboth said he would not give me his vineyard for any amount of money."

As her fingers gently settled on his head, she spoke in her softest, kindest voice.

"Oh, Ahab," she cooed, "you are the king, and no one can refuse the king. Naboth will give in to your request. I will see to it myself."

She excused herself, plotting as she quietly closed the door behind her. She knew this was an opportunity to punish another one of those useless Jews, and she fully intended to take it.

In her husband's chambers, she dipped his pen in black ink and began to write. When she finished the letter, she smiled cruelly, sealing it with the king's seal.

With her painted lips and her cold heart, she handed the letter off to a servant to take to the leaders where Naboth lived. She knew that they would accuse him of a crime he didn't commit, and it would eventually lead to his death.

She was right, of course, and the innocent Naboth was stoned so that Ahab could take over his vineyard. More than that, though, Jezebel had him killed so she could watch the fields of God wither and die, giving way to a place to plant more seeds for Baal.

Elijah, a prophet who spoke to the people about God, heard the news of Naboth's death and went to the palace immediately. He told the king what a horrific thing had been done and urged him to see how wrong it was. Ahab realized that what Elijah was saying was true, and he bent low in regret over the blood that had been spilled because of him.

Elijah warned him that Jezebel's heart was too wrapped in darkness to care about what she had done. She would die in the same place that Naboth had because the Lord was not going to allow her to go on destroying His people and His reputation.

Jezebel had never been afraid of Elijah before, and she wasn't going to start now. After all, what could his God do to her?

What Jezebel didn't consider was that God saw past all of her makeup and perfume.

She went on this way for years, but eventually it all caught up with her. Jehu the warrior had murdered her evil son, throwing his body into the field of Naboth, and now he was on his way to the palace to kill her.

And what do you think she did when she heard the news?

Well, the only thing she knew to do, of course: she painted on a beautiful face to hide her evil heart. She sat where she had on many mornings before, and she stained her lips blood-red to prepare for her death.

When the men got to the palace, she was looking out of the window from high above them, taunting them in her last moments. There was nothing about her that was good, and the men inside the palace knew it too.

Instead of protecting her, they flung open the window and threw her to the same ground that Naboth had died on, fulfilling the words of Elijah. After all of the damage she had done, and all of the terrible things she had caused, she died without defeating the One she wanted to destroy the most—the one true God.

Jezebel didn't want forgiveness from God; she wanted to use her scarlet mouth to speak lies about Him. Even in her death, she tried to cover her evil spirit with makeup and an expensive gown, pretending she was beautiful.

Ahab may have believed it, but God never did.

–from 1 Kings 21; 2 Kings 9

He

The Lord is **slow to anger**, which means He doesn't just react out of anger. Instead, every single day of our lives, He is patient beyond what we deserve. When He is angry at our behavior, it's because we have refused to obey Him. There isn't a single moment when you are doing everything perfectly, because you can't. In God's mercy, He doesn't punish us every time we do something wrong, and He restrains Himself from even being angry with us. But make no mistake: God has every right to be angry and to hold us responsible for our decisions.

Me

Have you ever been around someone who just wanted to be the center of attention and didn't care what anyone else wanted? It isn't a pretty sight. When we are inconsiderate and selfish, pushing ourselves into the spotlight and ignoring the people around us, it makes us the star instead of God. God wants us to have a quiet spirit and a gentle presence, where we are aware of others and thoughtful about allowing them time to speak and feel respected. Don't try to run people over with your personality to make sure that all eyes are on you. Instead, be kind and soft with your words, which will make sure that all eyes are where they're supposed to be: on God.

She

Lord, help _____ to remember that You are her audience, not the people around her (Galatians 1:10). Give her a strong and sensitive awareness of the people she is sharing her time with, and help her to be present with them and responsive to their words and needs. In her gentle presence, allow those around her to sense the spirit of God guiding her and giving her the affirmation that only You can. Let the compliments of others be insignificant compared to the joy that comes from pleasing You, and let her love for You drive her conversations and season every relationship she has.

*'**Anav** (ah NAHV) is the Hebrew word for "meek."*
The memory verse for this story is 1 Kings 21:29—
"I will not bring the disaster during his lifetime,
because he has humbled himself before Me."

Flour and Faith

The Story of the Widow of Zarephath

Long before Jezebel was thrown to her death, she had been warned by the prophet Elijah that Baal was not the real God. Still, people continued to believe that Baal was the god in charge of the storms. God wanted the people to see the truth, so He decided to show them Who was really in charge of the storms.

He told Elijah to go to Ahab and tell him that there was going to be a drought in the land.

"No rain will fall here," Elijah said to the king. "Not even mist will appear unless I command it to happen."

This was quite a claim, and Ahab shook his head. Who did this man think he was?

As the drought took its hold on the land, God took care of Elijah. He sent him to a brook where he would have water to drink. While he was there, the Lord also sent birds to bring him food. Eventually the brook dried up because there was no rain to fill it, and God sent Elijah on his next assignment.

"Now, go to a town called Zarephath, where I will have a woman feed you."
Elijah did exactly as he was commanded. When he came into the town, he
saw a woman gathering sticks and thought it must be her.

The woman's husband had died, so she was taking care of their son alone,
and she had very little money. In fact, she had nothing left at all for them to eat.

"Please, ma'am, may I have some water?"

The woman nodded and turned to fetch the pitcher, but before she walked
away, he had another request.

"And, also, a tiny bit of bread for me to eat, please."

She stopped cold and turned to face him.

"Sir, I have no bread in my house. In fact, with God as my witness, I tell you that I have only a handful of flour and a few drops of oil." Her face was tired and wet with tears. "The truth is that I have gathered these sticks so that my son and I may prepare our last bits of food and die. I have nothing left." She looked into Elijah's eyes desperately

"Go do as you have said you would," he replied. "But before you do that, make me a cake with the flour and oil."

She began to shake her head, wondering if he was a madman. Hadn't he heard a word she had said?

"Ma'am, your flour will not run out, nor will your oil. The Lord Himself will continue to fill the jars until it rains again."

It would seem that he really was a madman to make such a suggestion, but instead of questioning him, she simply turned and walked inside her house to do exactly as he had requested.

Just as Elijah had said, there was plenty of flour and oil for days. She could make no sense of it, but she gratefully continued to bake until the day when her son grew gravely ill.

His body was cold, and his breath was slow. Eventually, he stopped breathing altogether, and it became clear that he had died. She screamed at Elijah, blaming his God for her son's death.

Elijah was devastated. "Give him to me," he said and ran with the boy up to the room where he had been staying. He laid the boy on the bed, crying out to God to revive him.

"Lord, please don't take the boy. Let him live. Please, bring him back to life," he begged.

But who can bring a boy back from the dead? The widow knew he was gone, and she paced back and forth on the floor below them, wailing over the loss of her child.

She wasn't in the room when her son gasped and the air came back into him. She didn't see Elijah, pleading for the boy's life, nor did she know that God Himself had heard His servant's request.

As Elijah carried the widow's son back to her, his face pink with life, she knew Who could bring a boy back from the dead.

There had been nothing to offer—no baked bread and no way to make it.

But nothing was more than enough when it was given to a trustworthy God.

Faith in God can fill jars with flour and children with breath.

It can keep the sky from dropping rain to bring truth to a land of people who look in the wrong direction for a storm.

As Elijah handed the widow's son back into her shaking arms, he whispered to her, "See? He lives."

And in response, the woman nodded, knowing that it was true, that it was wonderful.

Yes, her boy lived.

But more than that, so does the God of Elijah.

—FROM 1 KINGS 17; 2 KINGS 4

He

Our God is **unchanging**. He is the same as He was yesterday, and He will still be the same in all our tomorrows and forevermore after that. His character never shifts, and He doesn't become a new personality or a different kind of God. He stays exactly as He is, which is one of the many reasons we can trust Him fully.

Me

No matter how little it seems like we have, God still wants us to live generously, always giving away what will help to build up people around us and bring glory to God. If we are faithful to do that, God won't leave us stranded. He loves it when we give away because we trust Him to take care of us. Nothing we own is really ours anyway, and we can show Him that we believe this in the way we share and give away.

She

Lord, let _____ be known for her generous spirit and the way she holds things of this world loosely (Colossians 3:2). Give her such a grateful and trusting heart that she is eager to help those around her from the excess of what You have given her. In the areas where she is more selfish and resistant to share, help her to genuinely recognize how little she deserves any of it, and how poorly it reflects on You when we greedily claim things as our own instead of giving all ownership to You. Let her be so consumed with the overflow of generosity You have shared that her immediate reaction to need is to recognize it as an opportunity and not a heavy obligation. Please give her the joy that comes with giving her life away.

Chazaq (khah ZAHK) is the Hebrew word for "constant."
The memory verse for this story is 1 Kings 17:16—
"The flour jar did not become empty, and the oil jug did not run dry, according to
the word of the Lord He had spoken through Elijah."

For Such a Time

The Story of Esther

The king had been humiliated by his wife. As punishment, he took the crown from Vashti and told her she would no longer be queen. He then requested that all women who were eligible to replace her to come to the palace at once.

King Ahasuerus had put his servant Hegai in charge of finding the most exquisite women in the land, and it was hard to imagine someone more beautiful than Esther. Along with several other women, Esther was chosen from the crowd to be brought into the palace, where they would spend a year preparing to meet the king.

Esther was Hegai's favorite, no question. He gave her the best of everything: makeup, food, and seven women to take care of her every need. But for all he knew about her, there was one thing he didn't.

She was a Jew.

Her cousin Mordecai had been very clear when she was chosen: *do not tell them anything about it*. Because so many people in Persia despised Jews, it could compromise her chances of being queen. So she obeyed him and didn't say a word.

She also listened to everything Hegai told her to do in order to please the king, never swaying from his advice. When the time finally came for her to be brought into the king's chambers, she walked slowly to him, her elegant dress perfectly fitted and her eyes warm with kindness.

He was overcome by her, and he loved her more than anyone else. Esther bowed her head for him to place her crown, and she became the queen of Persia.

One day after that, Mordecai was standing outside the palace gates, and he heard two of the king's servants discussing how they were going to kill the king. He immediately ran to Esther to tell her, and she warned the king before they succeeded. King Ahasuerus wrote down the name of the man who had saved his life so that he could thank him, but as time passed, the king forgot.

The king's assistant was a man named Haman, who was obsessed with power. In fact, Haman forced the people to bow down to him as if he were a god. They obeyed him, of course, because they didn't want to risk being in trouble with the king.

Well, all but one man obeyed him. Mordecai, a devout Jew, refused to bow to any god other than the true God. When all the other people knelt down to Haman, Mordecai stood tall on his feet. This made Haman furious, and he rushed into the palace with a plan to kill the Jews—*all of the Jews.*

Later, when Esther received a message from Mordecai, he told her that Haman had announced his evil plan, and he urged her to help. "You have to go to the king," he begged. "Don't let them kill all of us!"

Esther knew that she was not allowed to go to the king's chambers unless he requested her there. Going to him without an invitation was very dangerous, and the king could have her killed because of it.

"Mordecai," she responded, "you know what could happen to me." Esther realized she was going to have to risk her life to save her people.

"Esther, you are our only hope. What if you were chosen by God for such a time as this?" Mordecai asked.

The crown on her head may have been placed by human hands. But could it be that all along, God had known she would be here, at this very moment?

"Yes," she whispered. "I will go. If I die, I die." She told Mordecai to have all the Jews pray for her, and she set out to save her people.

It was a long, long walk to the king's chamber, and with every step, she had to remind herself to be courageous. She knew that when the king saw her, one of two things would happen: either he would lift his golden scepter for her to touch, accepting her in his presence, or he would not. If his scepter wasn't raised, she would be put to death.

Her hands shook as she watched the grand doors open, knowing this could be the end of her life. The king looked up and saw her walking slowly, just as she had the first time she met him. When she reached his throne, she bowed, waiting for her fate to be decided.

As soon as she did, the king raised his scepter for her to touch, giving her the freedom to speak. Her heart raced as she rested her fingers on the tip and invited the king and Haman to a special dinner, nodding gratefully when he accepted.

Haman was still reeling over the obstinate Mordecai, and he decided to have gallows made in order to hang Mordecai the next day.

But that night, the king couldn't sleep. He asked for his journals to be brought in to him, and he happened to go back to the page about the man who saved his life. He realized the man had never been rewarded, so he called in his advisors to discuss it.

"What do you think I should do for the man who was the most loyal to me?" he asked.

Haman was sure the king was talking about him, and he excitedly planned his own reward.

"I would treat him like a hero! Dress him in royal robes and parade him around on a horse so everyone can cheer for him and honor his greatness," Haman said.

He beamed at the king, waiting for his reward.

"Perfect," the king answered. "Do this for Mordecai the Jew, who has saved my life."

Mordecai? Haman's blood ran cold.

"Dinner is served!" called one of the servants.

Haman followed the king into the banquet room where Esther sat waiting. The following night, they had dinner again. The king offered Esther whatever she wished, and her words shocked the king.

"My lord, please rescue me from certain death. I am . . ." She paused to compose herself.

This was it.

117

"I am a Jew, sir. And an order has been sent out to have all of my people killed." She took a breath. "If it pleases you, will you call off the orders and protect us?"

Nobody would threaten the king's wife. Ahasuerus demanded to know who had made this decree.

"This wicked man," she answered, her delicate finger pointing to his assistant Haman.

And so, instead of being treated to the people's praise, Haman was sent to the gallows that he had built to kill Mordecai. Mordecai, on the other hand, was set on a horse and led around the town in the finest clothes money could buy.

Mordecai would become the king's new assistant and forevermore be revered as the man who stepped up to save his people after refusing to bow to anyone but God.

And Esther . . . beautiful Esther, the woman God used to protect His people.

She risked her life to make His name and His people great, and when the golden scepter was raised to offer her a voice, she knew the words of Mordecai were true: indeed, she had been chosen for a moment such as this.

—FROM THE BOOK OF ESTHER

He

God is **omnipotent**. He can do whatever He chooses to do. There is nothing that can beat Him and nothing that can overtake Him. He is strong enough to do anything He chooses, and His decisions cannot be overturned by anyone or anything else.

Me

Because of God's great power, we don't need to worry about our own weakness. When we step out in faith, choosing to believe that God is working through us instead of depending on us, we are free to live a life of courage. We don't have to be afraid that we aren't strong enough to do something or that we aren't big enough to take on challenges. Of course, we aren't strong or big when compared to God, but He is the One who carries our destinies. When we think we can't do something alone, it isn't weakness; it's realizing the truth. God is in charge, and trust me, that's exactly how we should want it to be.

She

Lord, help _____ to be courageous, always relying on Your power instead of her own (Joshua 1:7). When she comes up against a situation that looks terrifying, remind her that You don't see it through the same lens as she does and that You are at work in that exact moment. You never leave us, not for a second, and because of Your strength and overwhelming love for us, we don't need to let our lives be guided by our own assessments and estimations. Make it my constant goal to show her what a brave and God-trusting life looks like so that she will be quick to call on You in her times of doubt.

__Koach__ (KO ack) is the Hebrew word for "power."
The memory verse for this story is Esther 4:14—
"Who knows, perhaps you have come to your royal position
for such a time as this."

A Love Like This

The Story of Gomer

Hosea heard the voice of God commanding him to take a very unlikely woman as his wife, and he didn't hesitate to obey. He knew very well that there would be talk among the people when he married Gomer, but he trusted God.

He was a prophet, a man who shared a message given to him by God with the people, and she was a sinner whose life was marked by bad choices. Most people would say that she didn't deserve him, and maybe it was true, but it didn't matter. God had spoken, and Hosea listened.

Hosea fell deeply in love with his new bride, and when he thought he couldn't possibly care more about her, she whispered words that bent his heart in a new way: "We're going to have a baby."

Even though most people considered Gomer to be trash, Hosea saw something different. He wasn't as worried about her past as he was encouraged about her future, and he refused to give up on fighting for what she could be one day.

As her belly grew, so did the rumors.

Do you know where she came from?

A woman like that could never change.

She's a liar and a cheat, and she's going to do it over and over again.

But Hosea wouldn't hear it. Gomer was his wife, and he would honor and defend her as long as he lived.

Their son was born, and laughter filled their house. And for a while, all was well.

But eventually Gomer started to remember the way her life used to be, and she started to miss it. The old life wasn't great; she knew that. But sometimes she thought that running away and being free to do whatever she wanted would be easier than being true to her husband.

And even when she wandered back to her old friends and everyone tried to convince Hosea she was useless, he stood his ground.

She had two more babies, and Hosea didn't even know for sure that he was their father. But he chose to love her and be faithful to her anyway.

One day Gomer decided she was finished with him and with her life there. Hosea was devastated when he found out she had run away. He had always dreamed that he would make her happy and she would change her ways for good, but now she was gone forever.

Well, he thought she was.

But the voice of the Lord came again to him, this time telling Hosea to go and rescue his wife from the life she was living.

It may have crossed his mind that she didn't love him anymore, that she probably didn't want anything to do with him. But God was clear: *This is not about her love for you; it's about your love for her. Go and save her.*

Hosea knew she had become a slave, so he went to the town where she was living to try to find her. And when he did, his heart broke all over again.

She was hardly the woman he remembered. Filthy, desperate, and hopeless, she stood silently as the men around her asked who wanted to buy her. Not that anyone would pay much for her—she was trash, remember?

But who can explain a love like this?

Hosea saw her dirty skin and tired eyes, and he knew she was far away from God. But he saw more than that, and he raised his hand proudly until the bidding was done and she was brought to him.

"Gomer, you were meant for more than this," he whispered tenderly. "Come with me, my bride, and let me take care of you forever."

Her eyes began to come to life again, and she shook her head. How could he love her after all she had done?

But he did.

He does.

He always will.

Just like Gomer, the Israelites had wandered far, far away from God many times. His love for them was undeniable, and yet it never satisfied them. So they tried to go back to the mistakes, back to the darkness, back to the place where they were slaves.

But God would not allow it.

Even when it didn't make sense, He chased them. And when anyone else would have said they weren't worth it, He still chose to call them *His*.

He calls *us* His.

From the garden until the end of time, He has made us the object of His affection. His strong arms reach us no matter where we are, holding us to Himself and reminding us that we were made for more.

Do we deserve it? No, we don't. And have we done things that were wrong? Of course we have.

And yet, He finds us in the rubble and raises His hand to claim us. God Himself—the creator of the stars and the seas and the wind and the days— He calls us His bride, and He rescues us.

Who can explain a love like this?

—FROM THE BOOK OF HOSEA

124

He

Even when we aren't faithful to God, He is **faithful** to us. What does that mean? It means He will never stop keeping His promises to us. Even if we break our word and act in ways that are wrong, it won't change the promises He has made to us.

Me

Because of the great mercy that God has shown to us, we should also be people who show mercy. When someone wrongs us, hurts our feelings, or breaks our hearts, we have to remember that Christ Himself died out of His great mercy, and these are small things compared to those. The way we teach people about forgiveness is by forgiving them. And when we show mercy, we are telling them that we have no right to hold their wrongs against them because God didn't hold ours against us.

She

Lord, make _____'s heart tender with Your mercy (Micah 6:8), and let that gratitude serve her well and give her great empathy for sin and appreciation for grace. When things go wrong and her temptation is to withhold her forgiveness, remind her that You didn't, and that her mercy opens the door for greater understanding of Yours. Let her rest in the steady foundation of Your faithfulness, relying on Your wrath and understanding of justice more than her own.

*'**Aman** (ah MAN) is the Hebrew word for "faithful."*
The memory verse for this story is Hosea 1:10 ESV—
"And in the place where it was said to them, 'You are not my people,'
it shall be said to them, 'Children of the living God.'"

Just a Girl

The Story of Mary and Elizabeth, Both with Child

Zechariah and his wife Elizabeth didn't have any children, and they had given up on trying a long time ago. If that was what God had decided was best for them, they were at peace.

One day, Zechariah entered the temple to perform his priestly duties, and he saw something that made his heart skip a beat. He stood still, looking at what appeared to be an angel standing next to the altar of the temple. He trembled in fear, but the angel spoke kindly to him.

"It's all right, Zechariah," the angel Gabriel said. "I have come to share good news with you."

Zechariah stared at him, trying to understand what was happening.

"Your wife Elizabeth is going to have a son, and he won't be just an ordinary boy," Gabriel explained. "You will name him John, and you should know this: he will prepare the way for the Son of God."

Zechariah shook his head in doubt.

"I'm just an old man," Zechariah answered. "I don't see how this could work."

Because Zechariah didn't believe what he was hearing, God took his voice from him, and Gabriel told him he wouldn't be able to speak for some time. The people praying outside the temple wondered what was taking Zechariah so long, and they began to worry about him. When he finally came out, he looked frightened and pointed to his mouth to show them he couldn't make a sound.

They knew he must have seen something of God in there.

Just as the angel had predicted, Elizabeth became pregnant. She thanked God for giving her a baby. Little did she know that the same angel who had come to her husband would also speak to her cousin Mary, and their lives were about to be woven together in a most incredible way.

Mary was a young woman, engaged to be married to a carpenter named Joseph. There didn't seem to be anything extraordinary about her; she wasn't wealthy or powerful or even from a famous town.

She was just a girl.

But God had chosen her to bring the world the most important person who would ever live.

Gabriel came to Mary's house in Nazareth to tell her what was going to happen. As soon as she saw him, she became nervous the way Zechariah had. The angel reassured her that everything was going to be fine, and he began to explain that God had chosen her for a very special role.

Mary's hands shook as she listened to the angel.

"You will have a son, and His name will be Jesus," he said. "He will be the Son of God, the One who was promised so long ago. And His kingdom will never, ever end."

She was wide-eyed and confused, knowing that she could hardly have a baby when she wasn't even married yet.

"How?" she whispered, trying to understand.

"It may seem impossible to you, but God can do anything," Gabriel explained. "And your cousin Elizabeth? The one who has never been able to have a baby? Well, she's pregnant too."

Mary didn't know how all of this would happen, but unlike Zechariah, she believed God could do whatever He wanted to do. She bowed low to the angel with tears in her eyes.

"I am the Lord's; let it happen however He chooses," she said to Gabriel. And with that, the angel left.

Mary hurried to get her things together, setting out for the hill country of Judah to see Elizabeth. It took her several days to get there, and as soon as she walked into Elizabeth's house, she called out for her dear cousin.

When she did, the baby in Elizabeth's belly jumped. Immediately, Elizabeth knew something amazing had happened.

She stared at Mary, shocked by what God had revealed to her.

"Your baby!" Elizabeth shouted joyfully. "I know who He is!" Elizabeth's face grew pale as she considered how close she was to the holiness of God Himself.

"What have I done to deserve being near to you, the one chosen as the mother of our Lord?" Elizabeth asked her cousin.

"Elizabeth, I'm just a girl. There's nothing special about me," Mary said. "But God has asked for my obedience, and I have given it to Him." She began to thank God for all the wonderful things He had already done, and while the baby kicked and wiggled inside her, Mary praised Him for what was to come.

Mary stayed with Elizabeth for three more months and eventually went home as she neared the day of Jesus' birth.

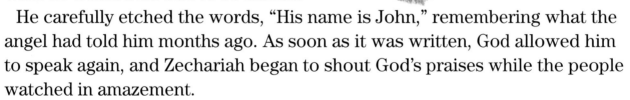

The time came for Elizabeth to have her baby, and when she delivered him, she told her friends and relatives that his name would be John. Everyone around her thought he should be named Zechariah after his father. Because Zechariah couldn't talk, they passed him a writing tablet and asked him what he wanted his son to be named.

He carefully etched the words, "His name is John," remembering what the angel had told him months ago. As soon as it was written, God allowed him to speak again, and Zechariah began to shout God's praises while the people watched in amazement.

"My son will make a way for the One . . ." he began, his voice cracking. "For the One who will make a way for all of us!"

Zechariah looked at his newborn baby, sleeping in Elizabeth's arms.

"It is finally happening," he said in a hushed voice, glancing at the crowd around him. "We are going to be rescued, and the light from His life will flood the darkness forever."

They could see it in his eyes—it was the truth. The sin that had followed them from the garden until now would finally be overcome through one child: *Jesus*. God, in His mercy, was going to send them a Redeemer.

—FROM LUKE 1

He

God is **perfect**, meaning there is nothing wrong with Him, He doesn't make mistakes, and there is nothing in His character that isn't exactly as it should be. As humans, we can never actually be perfect, but our goal is to always try to be as much like God as we can be.

Me

As children of God, we need to be willing to be used by Him in the ways that He decides are best. They may not always be what seems easiest or best to us, but because we love and trust God, we surrender to Him. Another word for that is *submissive*, which means we are more worried about doing what He wants us to do than we are with our own plans.

She

Lord, help _____ to have a submissive spirit (1 Peter 5:6), one that always seeks Your will over her own. When You ask her to lay down her life, in whatever ways You will, make her a willing conduit of Your plan. As she grows spiritually, anchor her in Your Word and the study of Your characteristics and truths so that she will be more and more like You every day.

Teleios (TE lay os) is the Greek word for "perfect."
The memory verse for this story is Luke 1:37—
"For nothing will be impossible with God."

The Sacred Ordinary

The Story of Mary and the Birth of Christ

*M*ary's belly was full of baby, and she knew she was getting close to the day she would finally meet her son.

"We have to go, Mary," Joseph said. "We really don't have a choice. It'll take us several days to get there, but I'll do all I can to make it comfortable for you."

Caesar Augustus wanted to know how many people there were in his empire, and the best way to count all the people was to have them return to their hometowns. For Joseph and Mary, that meant riding their donkeys eighty miles from Nazareth to Joseph's hometown of Bethlehem.

They saddled up the donkeys and began traveling with all the others who were heading that way. Once they reached Bethlehem, Mary was sure of one thing.

The baby was coming.

"Joseph," she whispered, "it's almost time."

They hurried to the nearest inn to find a room, but the innkeeper shook his head. There was no room, and time was short. Joseph took Mary to the place were the animals were kept because there was no room anywhere else. Mary delivered baby Jesus there.

As soon as the child was born, Mary gently wrapped Him in blankets and held Him closely to her chest. Joseph reached for her face, tenderly wiping the sweat from her flushed cheeks.

And there, near the braying donkey and the straw-covered ground, the Savior of the world breathed in the night air for the first time. His fingers opened and closed slowly, and His heart beat like His mother's. *Like ours.*

He slept in peace while the angels sang praise in a nearby field, telling the shepherds of His birth.

"The Christ is here," the angels declared. "He has been born!" A bright light shone around them while the shepherds stared into the great holy.

Other than Joseph and Mary, they were the first on earth to know.

Not the kings and queens or the wealthiest and most famous people in the land. Not the religious leaders or the most powerful rulers. He could have been born anywhere, in any number of ways that would have commanded attention, but He wasn't.

"You will find Him in a manger wrapped in swaddling clothes," the angels continued. "He is the promised One."

The angels disappeared, and the shepherds knew they must go and find Him. As they entered Bethlehem, they came upon the humble place where the animals were kept and saw a man and a woman holding a newborn baby. The baby was swaddled in cloth exactly as the angels had said He would be, and the shepherds fell to their knees in awe.

"Angels came to us," they said, "and they told us of the child."

Tears spilled onto Mary's cheeks as she listened to the first words spoken about her son.

"He is the One we have been waiting for," they whispered.

High in the night sky, a star moved steadily toward the stable, guiding the wise men to where He was. They followed it eagerly, knowing it was leading them to the Christ child. For many weeks they traveled underneath the star until it finally settled in Bethlehem above the house where Mary and Joseph were. As they entered the house, their knees bent in reverence.

"Blessed King of David," they cried, "we have come to worship You and offer You gifts." They placed gold, frankincense, and myrrh near the child, their eyes tracing the outline of His small body in Mary's arms.

Everything that had gone wrong with the world would be made right through this child. His face was pink, His hair was damp and dark in color, and His eyes were blinking as He looked around the small room. His tiny chest rose and fell softly, the Holy being filled with the breath of humanity.

Jesus.

For now, the best Mary and Joseph could do was to keep Him warm and fed, to rock Him gently to sleep, and to sing praises over Him while He rested. With every passing day they watched as He grew like any other child, His feet outgrowing His sandals while He learned to feed Himself and to speak the words they taught Him.

It wasn't the way many people expected the Savior to come into the world, but that's exactly why it happened the way it did. From His first cry in the manger, God wanted us to know that He was like us.

Or rather, *that we were like Him.*

One young woman.

One *yes*.

One manger in a small town.

One baby who brought the peace of God to the people of the world.

One night where the ordinary kissed the sacred, never to be the same again.

—FROM LUKE 2

He

God is **gracious**, meaning that He loves to give us the things we don't deserve. He delights in lavishing His goodness on us, and it is His good and perfect will to do that in whatever ways He chooses as best. In His Son Jesus, God gave us the greatest gift of grace the world would ever know, and He continues to bless us even though we haven't earned a right to His favor.

Me

We are called to be holy, which means that the patterns of our thoughts, decisions, and actions should be as close to God's as possible. He wants our lives to be pure and clean, refusing to let the filth of the world change us or make us look less like Him.

She

Lord, give _____ a keen discernment for the things of the world that affect her journey to holiness (Romans 12:1). As she grows in the Word and in knowledge of You, make the stench of sin so strong that her first reaction is to run from it, rebuke it, and refuse to take part in it. Lead her to people who have also made this their goal, so they can help and encourage each other and remind one another of the very high standards of God. And when she fails, remind her of Your grace quickly so that she doesn't lose heart over her mistakes.

__Hagios__ (HAHG ee os) is the Greek word for "holy."
The memory verse for this story is Luke 2:10–11 ESV—
"Fear not, for behold, I bring you good news of great joy that will be for all the people.
For unto you is born this day in the city of David a Savior,
who is Christ the Lord."

The Lamb

The Story of Anna

$\mathcal{A}$nna knelt behind the group of people who had come to the temple, her fingers looped together in prayer.

She had been doing this every single day since she lost her husband many, many years before. She had only been married for seven years when he died, and she had decided that instead of remarrying, she would spend her life completely focused on God.

When the sun came up each morning, she was awake and already praying for the day. She made her way into the temple before anyone else was there and settled into her familiar spot. Every day brought different people and situations to pray about, but underneath all of her words was the longing of her heart.

More than anything else in this world, Anna wanted to see the promised One before she died. She believed that He was coming, and as the hours of her life ticked past, she wondered if God would grant her request.

Many babies were brought to the temple by their mothers to be presented to the Lord, and when this happened, the baby's mother was also supposed to bring a lamb and a pigeon to offer to God. Some of the people who came didn't have enough money for a lamb, so they were allowed to bring another pigeon instead.

Either way, Anna prayed for every child.

It became harder and harder to kneel on the floor as her legs grew weak with age, but she never stopped doing it. Oftentimes she would even refuse to eat because she felt like it distracted her from her prayers.

When the moonlight poured into the temple, she would reach for a steady piece of furniture, slowly lifting herself up and walking into the night.

Maybe tomorrow, she would think.

And when she would finally fall into her bed, closing her eyes to rest, her thoughts would chase the possibility until her dreams brought her to daylight again.

Anna knew the only thing that really mattered was the One who was going to make things right for the people of Israel. After all, she believed God was real and that He was going to give them a Redeemer.

Her ears didn't hear all the sounds they used to, and her eyes couldn't see all that well. Her bones were creaky and tired, and her fingers ached from bending, but she ignored all of it.

She heard things from God in ways that most people couldn't. She hurried to get dressed, her wrinkled hands tying her clothes into place while her heart raced. She knew that today might be the day she saw the promised Messiah.

She hurried to get dressed, her wrinkled hands wrestling the buttons into place while her heart raced.

The child was coming.

All the years, all the prayer, all the offerings and pleading—it had been for this moment.

She walked quickly, guided by the very presence of God, and when she entered the temple, she heard a familiar voice echoing from the walls. Simeon, a great man of God, had arrived just before her.

Standing beside Simeon were a woman and a man, both staring at Simeon as he spoke. And there, inside the temple where she had spent so many days and nights, she finally saw the baby in Simeon's arms: the baby born to save the world.

"I can die in peace now," said Simeon, his weak arms holding Strength. "My eyes have seen Him."

And there beside the altar were two pigeons, brought by Mary and Joseph because they could not afford a lamb.

Anna burst into praise and began telling everyone what she had seen.

She had waited all this time to see His tiny arms, the arms that would grow to stretch from one side of a cross to another so that we could be His again.

Soon there would be no need for sacrifices at the temple anymore because Jesus Himself would be the offering.

Mary and Joseph had made their way to Jerusalem with only two pigeons, but soon the world would know the truth of Anna's words:

The baby in Simeon's arms was the very Lamb of God.

—from Luke 2

He

God has never made a **promise** that He won't keep—it's impossible. He tells us in the book of Genesis that He will never again flood the earth, and He won't. We can rest in that and not give it another thought. Or when He tells Abraham that he will have a son in his old age, as ridiculous as it seems, He will see it through (and He did—see Genesis). If God has promised it, it will happen; that's all there is to it.

Me

One of the main ways we can learn more about the heart of God and develop a relationship with Him is through prayer. Being prayerful is so important, and it doesn't just mean that you say a few words before you climb in your bed at night or right before you eat your food. Those things are wonderful, but even more than that, God wants you to have a prayerful life, always thinking of Him, speaking to Him, and inviting Him into your daily life and experiences.

She

Lord, cultivate a disciplined prayer life in _____ (James 5:16). Let her conversations, requests, and doubts weave a beautiful life that is hidden in Your promises and Your love for her. Let her not grow weary when she doesn't feel like she is seeing the fruit of her requests; only steady her up in patience and remind her that You will see every detail through. Remind her that nothing has been left to chance.

__Epaggelia__ (ep angh el EE ah) is the Greek word for "promise."
The memory verse for this story is Luke 2:38—
"At that very moment, she came up and began to thank God and to speak about Him
to all who were looking forward to the redemption of Jerusalem."

An Empty Pitcher

The Story of the Woman at the Well

She liked to go to the well in the heat of the day because she knew it wouldn't be crowded. That way, she didn't have to answer everyone's questions or look away from people's icy stares. She knew what they thought about her, and she would rather pretend none of it existed.

I would rather face the blazing sun than their faces, she thought. Sweat rolled down her back as she reached the well. There was a man there whom she had never seen before, and she avoided His gaze the same way she did everyone else's.

"Give Me a drink," the man said.

The woman knew that He was a Jew and wasn't supposed to talk to Samaritans like herself. She asked Him why He would ask such a thing of a woman He shouldn't even be speaking to.

"If you knew who you were talking to right now, you would have asked Him for living water," the man answered, "and He would have given it to you."

The woman was puzzled and looked around Him for an explanation.

"You don't have a bucket, a rope, or anything else to lower into this well," she answered. "It's incredibly deep, so I don't know how You think You would manage to get water."

He looked at her kindly, and she wasn't sure what to make of Him.

"This water will quench your thirst for a little while," He said, "but there's another kind of water you can drink if you never want to be thirsty again."

"I want that water," she said. "Give it to me so I won't have to keep coming here day after day."

The man told her to go and get her husband, and she shook her head in response. "I don't have a husband," she said.

"No," the man answered calmly. "You don't. But you have had five husbands already, and the man you spend time with now isn't your husband."

She stared at Him, her lip quivering in shock.

"You . . . ," she began, "You must be a prophet. How could You know all of that?"

Her empty water pitcher sat beside her as she forgot the reason she had come in the first place.

"I believe the Messiah is coming," she told Him, "and when He comes to us, He's going to explain everything. He's going to make things right."

Nothing in the world could have prepared her for what He was about to say.

"I am that man," He whispered.

She knew it was true; how else could He have known everything about her? She stumbled over her feet, running as fast as she could into the town to tell everyone about Him. Now, instead of avoiding those who judged her, she was trying to find them.

God had come down to save sinners just like her, and not even her own shame could keep her from telling them. With her pitcher left behind her at the well, she shouted about what had just happened to anyone who would listen.

The baby Jesus had grown to be a man. His cousin John had baptized Him exactly as it had been predicted, and now He was traveling with a group of men to share the good news with people everywhere.

147

For so many years, God's people had ignored Him. But He kept loving them and kept trying to show them that He was real. And when Jesus came to earth, He found a woman who had ignored God for years as well.

It would be easy to imagine that God would send His Son to live in a palace on earth and to demand that all the important people pay attention to Him. After all, He could have come any way He wanted.

But Jesus had been born alongside the soft noises of animals in a manger. And when the time came for Him to announce who He was, it was to a woman who was running away from her mistakes.

Why? Well, because He wanted her to run toward the town while praising Him, instead of running away from it in shame.

She thought she was going to fill her pitcher, but instead she left with a promise that couldn't be contained.

The Messiah had finally come.

—FROM JOHN 4

He

The Lord is **near** to you, even in this very moment. Even though you can't see Him or touch Him, He is all around you—in front of you and behind you. He is a God who loves His people so much that He makes Himself near even though He could have stayed far away forever. He chooses this because He wants to have a relationship with you, and He wants you to experience His presence even though you can't see Him.

Me

We should pray to be discerning, meaning that we have a sense of what God is doing in and through other people. You can ask God to help you to see when someone might not have your best in mind, or even when there might be a person around you who needs a kind word or deed. Ask Him to help you recognize good and bad in others and to act when He invites you to speak into their lives.

She

Lord, may _____ always have a strong sense of Your presence and Your accessibility. As she speaks to You, help her to develop a strong discernment so that she will begin to see people as You see them (Hebrews 4:13). As she learns to trust Your voice more and more, continue to guide her to godly people and opportunities that will remind her of the desires of Your heart for her.

Diakrisis (dee AK re sis) is the Greek word for "discern."
The memory verse for this story is John 4:14—
"But whoever drinks from the water that I will give him
will never get thirsty again—ever!"

The Hem

The Story of the Woman with an Illness

It had been twelve long years of suffering, and her illness wasn't getting any better.

She had been to many doctors, but they all shook their heads when she asked what could be done.

She had no money left, and she was desperate.

The voices grew louder, and the crowds pushed until she could hardly see where she was going. But she didn't stop walking. They were all following the same man, so as long as she could keep up with them, there was a chance she would get to Him.

She kept her head low, knowing that she wasn't even allowed to be out in public like this, let alone trying to get near a man like Jesus. People with her illness were supposed to stay inside and away from everyone else. She was considered second class—a nuisance and a reject.

She knew what they would think when they saw her, and they were probably right. *Who in the world does she think she is, anyway?* But something told her it was going to be different this time, and more than anything else, she simply believed that Jesus could make her well.

In fact, she believed so much in His power that she didn't even think He had to see her in order to heal her. So when the crowd parted enough for her to see the hem of His robe, she didn't think twice. She jumped forward, and as all the people crowded around her, she reached her hand out and touched His garment.

In that instant, she was made well.

The sickness that a dozen years and doctors and medicine couldn't fix was gone the moment her fingers wrapped around the fabric.

She knew it, of course. She felt it right away.

And I'm sure she would have run away rejoicing, had it not been for the voice she heard next.

"Who touched My garments?" He asked.

Jesus Himself was speaking, and she knew that if He could make her well, He could certainly figure out who had touched Him.

The disciples made a fuss, saying, "There are people everywhere! Of course you are being touched. You're surrounded by a crowd!"

But Jesus knew this was different, and so did the woman.

Silence swallowed the crowd as she stepped forward.

Who in the world does she think she is?

She felt her whole body shaking as she bowed low before Him, unsure of what her punishment might be. She told Him the truth—the whole story—from the beginning. She explained who she was and what had happened.

The most beautiful part of all was that He listened. The crowd would have liked to move Him along, but He made time for her, just as He does for you. And when she finished, He said only a few words to her, but they were such wonderful words.

He told her that she was healed.

Although he wanted her to hear Him, He also wanted the people around to hear. He didn't want them to be confused about what had happened.

Yes, Jesus had the power to heal her, but it wasn't her fingers that made it happen.

It was her faith.

Jesus wanted everyone to see her the way He did. She wasn't just another face in the crowd to Him, and she wasn't just a woman who should be sent away because she was dirty.

He had called her "daughter," and that's exactly the message He wanted to send to everyone there that day.

This girl who you think is nothing? She's Mine.

And the way she believed in Me made her well.

Not just in her body, but in her soul, where it really matters.

Who do you think you *are?*

Before you turn the page, I hope you will ask the same question, just so you can hear His voice, louder than any other in the crowd.

He waits while you speak, because you're worth listening to. And then a hush comes as He smiles at you like you're the only one in the world.

And with one word, He says everything.

"Daughter . . ."

—FROM LUKE 8

He

The Lord is a **healer**, and He is the only One who can heal us in the way we most need it: by paying for our sin and bringing us close to God the Father. Even if things look hopeless, it might just mean that God hasn't had His final say yet, and there are no amount of medical tests or sicknesses that can overpower God's will.

Me

It is important to be zealous for God's Word and for God Himself. We can't get lazy or stop being interested in learning His ways—we should always be growing more like Him. God doesn't want His people to stop being curious or to think they have figured Him out. They haven't, because they can't. There is always more and more and more to know about God, and that should keep us excited and active in our search.

She

Lord, make _____ a zealous follower of Yours (Titus 2:14) so that others can see the light of life You have put in her and sustained. Make her a passionate reader of Your Word and an eager learner when it comes to matters of faith. May she never have apathy toward the things that matter most to You, and may she always be driven by compassion, gratitude, and a keen awareness of everything close to Your heart.

Therapeuō (ther ap YOO oh) is the Greek word for "heal."
The memory verse for this story is Luke 8:48—
"Daughter," He said to her, "your faith has made you well. Go in peace."

$\mathcal{A}rise$

The Story of Jairus's Daughter

$\mathcal{J}$ust before Jesus' attention had turned to the woman who touched his hem, a man had also made his way to Jesus.

Jesus had arrived by boat, and He had hardly set foot on dry land when Jairus came running up to Him. Jairus wasn't just an ordinary man. He was a ruler in his church, looked up to and respected by the people.

As he fell down at Jesus' feet, the people heard him crying and begging for help.

"My daughter," he cried, "she is nearly dead."

Everyone looked to Jesus. He was the miracle-maker after all.

"I know that You can heal her if You will just come with me and lay Your hands on her." As soon as Jairus finished speaking, the Lord began to walk with him in the direction of his house.

I imagine Jairus was racing, desperate to get there before time ran out.

It was at this moment that the sick woman reached out to Jesus, and I wonder if Jairus panicked as he listened to the conversation between them. In a house not very far away was his precious little girl, fighting to stay alive.

He never said that his daughter was more important than this woman, but it had to be obvious to everyone there.

The daughter of such an important man should have priority over this filthy, sick woman. And yet Jesus didn't seem to care. He was nodding, listening, spending precious time with that woman when He should have been tending to the child of a ruler instead.

While Jesus and the woman were still speaking, a man ran toward Jairus and said, "Why bother Jesus anymore? Your daughter is dead. She's dead! It's too late now."

Jesus heard him, and He looked at Jairus, eye to eye.

"Don't be afraid. Just believe," Jesus said calmly.

They walked together until they arrived at Jairus's house, where people were gathered together, weeping and screaming because the girl had died.

Jesus wanted them to believe the way the woman had, but they didn't. In fact, when He told them that she was only sleeping, they laughed at Him.

Jesus went inside the house, taking Jairus and his wife along with three of His disciples. He walked over to the little girl, took her hand, and whispered, "Little girl, I say to you, arise."

Everyone watched in amazement as the girl stood to her feet immediately and began to walk like she had never been sick at all. But those who saw it with their own eyes knew that she had been dead and was now alive, and they knew who had made it so.

The girl was twelve years old, the same number of years that the woman who had touched Jesus' garment had suffered with her sickness. One was a commoner, and the other was an innocent child born to a man that mattered. And yet, Jesus saw them both as valuable.

He didn't look at people the way everyone else did, with everything on the outside distracting them. Jesus wanted the people to know that faith is what made them beautiful.

These two girls had more in common than being healed on the same day.

They were both daughters . . .

Of a very, *very* important man.

Arise, Love. Your Father has spoken.

—FROM LUKE 8

He

God is a **miracle-maker**, and nothing is ever too far gone for Him to bring it back to Himself. No rebellion or sickness or destruction can ever be too terrible for God to restore. His power is even greater than death.

Me

Often when we hear the word *meek*, we think it means weakness, but it doesn't. It's actually a form of strength, where we use self-control to keep us from acting like we're the bosses when we're not. It means that we are listening to God more than ourselves and we are acting in ways that line up with His desires. We aren't barreling through life making our own demands and decisions. Rather we are being patient in spirit and gentle at heart so we leave plenty of room for God to be the star of our lives.

She

Lord, let _____ find joy in being a girl who has a meek and lowly spirit (Psalm 22:26), deferring to Your ways instead of her own. Help her to see the ways that she might be ignoring or unaware of Your voice, and continue to affirm Yourself as her strong foundation instead of applause, compliments, threats, fears, or any other desire that is based on the world and not on You. Give her the confidence to pray for miracles and the hope that comes from believing that You are exactly who You say You are.

***Sēmeion** (say MAY on) is the Greek word for "miracle."*
The memory verse for this story is Luke 8:54—
"So He took her by the hand and called out, 'Child, get up!'"

Platter

The Story of Salome and Herodias

King Herod was used to getting what he wanted. And in this case, that meant his brother's wife. He didn't care if it was wrong, and he wasn't concerned with his own wife either. He would just divorce her and marry Herodias instead.

So he did.

When John the Baptist heard what the king had done, he was horrified. He immediately confronted the king about his wrongdoing and told him that it was terrible and unlawful.

Herod actually respected John and listened to his words. But Herod's new wife, well, that was another matter. She insisted that Herod throw John in prison for speaking out against their marriage, and she began to plan a worse punishment for him as well.

As far as she was concerned, John should be dead. If Herod kept listening to John, there was a chance he would eventually believe him, and Herodias couldn't stand that idea.

Like her husband, nothing was off-limits when she wanted something.

Herodias and her first husband had a daughter named Salome, and one night Salome was invited to dance for the king and his friends. Herod was so enchanted with Salome that he told her he would give her anything she wanted. So Salome went to her mother and explained what had happened.

"He said *anything*, Mother. Up to half his kingdom," she said. "And he didn't just say he would give it to me—he gave his solemn promise that he would."

Herodias smiled wickedly while Salome continued.

"Mother, what should I ask for?"

Herodias didn't even take a breath before she answered. She had waited for this opportunity for a long time, and her anger spilled out in one sentence that would bring the death of a good man.

"Tell him," she whispered coyly, "that you want the head of John the Baptist on a plate, and you want it *now*."

Herodias watched her daughter turn back to King Herod, telling him that she had made up her mind. Herod was stuck. He didn't want to do it, but all the people were watching him. After all, he had promised Salome that he would do what she asked.

So he told the guards to go and kill John, and they soon brought his head up and gave it to Salome. She carried it to her mother, who was delighted that John the Baptist was finally dead.

The followers of Christ buried John's body and went to tell Jesus that His cousin was gone. He was terribly sad to hear the news, and He walked ahead of the others so He could spend some time alone praying.

Despite all of her scheming and tantrums, the best reward Herodias got was the death of an innocent man. John, on the other hand, would spend eternity with the God he had faithfully served on earth.

In all her wickedness, Herodias had killed one of the messengers. But unfortunately for her, she could never stop the message.

—FROM MARK 6

He

God is our great **Defender**, and there is no person or thing that can beat us when He is standing in front of us. He is a mighty shield, and He goes ahead of us, follows behind us, and is always in the midst of all our battles. He will not only protect you, but He will also fight for you (Exodus 14:14), which means you don't have to rely on your own strength to succeed.

Me

Many times, you will want to take a situation into your own hands and make sure that the people who have hurt or upset you are properly punished. The problem is, you aren't anywhere near as capable to do that as God is. Don't be a controller, always looking to make things look right to you; instead, pray that you would be reliant on God, trusting that He always makes things right.

She

Jesus, give _____ a clear and constant faith in Your willingness and ability to go to battle on her behalf (Deuteronomy 1:30). When things happen that don't seem to make sense, remind her that You are still our High Priest and great Defender, interceding and fighting for us. Calm her fears when she feels cornered and weak, giving her Your strength in place of hers.

Phimoō (fee MOH oh) is the Greek word for "be still."
The memory verse for this story is Mark 6:22—
"Ask me whatever you want, and I'll give it to you."

Crumbs

The Story of the Gentile Mother

She saw Jesus in the distance and ran toward Him, knowing she was taking a risk.

"Please," she begged, "have mercy on me!"

The men around Jesus stared at her, wondering what He would do to this Canaanite woman. Her ancestors wanted nothing to do with God, so what right did she have to speak to the Son of God? It was ridiculous.

"Sir!" she yelled, moving closer to Him as her voice grew louder. "It's my daughter. She has been taken over by demons. Please heal her!"

Jesus did nothing.

The disciples were furious, and they told Jesus to send her away.

"She won't leave us alone!" they complained.

Jesus finally spoke, "I have come to save the lost sheep of the house of Israel."

Yes, the disciples thought, *not nuisances like her*.

But the woman would not give up. She ran in front of Him and fell to her knees to stop Him from walking.

"Lord. Please," she cried. "Please help me."

"It isn't right to take the children's bread and throw it to dogs," He said.

She understood what He was saying: God's chosen people were the Israelites, and she wasn't an Israelite. In fact, she was considered no better than a dog to many of the Jews. They didn't think she deserved to be helped the way that they did, and it seemed like Jesus agreed.

The disciples waited for Him to humiliate her and push her out of the way, but He didn't.

He listened.

"Yes, Lord," she said quietly. "But even the dogs eat crumbs that fall from their masters' table." She didn't deny that she was a Gentile, a non-Jew, but she urged Him to help her anyway.

That's the part that mattered the most to Jesus. He could see that she believed He was exactly who He said He was. And it was that faith that made her one of God's people, not the family she was born into here on earth.

She couldn't help but beg Him because she believed He had enough power for all the Jews and Gentiles who believed in Him.

And as the disciples shook their stubborn heads and made fun of the woman who had bothered them, Jesus looked at her tenderly and answered her in love.

"Your faith is wonderful. Because of it, your daughter is being healed as we speak," He said.

And she was.

All because one woman dared to believe that Jesus the promised Christ had come to the world with enough power to save *anyone* who asked to be healed.

—FROM MARK 7

He

God is **incomprehensible**, which means that no matter how much we do learn about Him, we can never understand everything. Because He is perfect and we aren't, we weren't made in a way that can fully comprehend Him. He gives us enough to know what we need to in order to trust, love, and obey Him, but there will never be a day in this life that we figure out all of His mysteries.

Me

Always try to be thoughtful, considering the motives and needs of others. Don't just act out of your own needs or wants, but think about what the people around you might need. If you've said something hurtful or done something that caused another person sadness, apologize and do it differently next time. In every situation, make sure you are paying attention to how the other people might be feeling, and ask God to give you wisdom in knowing how to help.

She

Lord, give _____ such a genuine affection for people that her immediate response is based not only on herself, but on them as well (Philippians 2:4). Give her a supernatural awareness of people's needs and clear direction when there is something You want to speak through her. Let her stand in awe of Your mystery because she is so settled in her faith, overwhelmed by Your majesty and convinced of Your character.

Mystērion (moo STAY ree on) is the Greek word for "mystery."
The memory verse for this story is Mark 7:28—
"Lord, even the dogs under the table eat the children's crumbs."

The First Stone

The Story of the Adulterous Woman

They pushed her roughly in front of them, paying no attention to her shame-filled pleading. She had been caught with a man who wasn't her husband, and the religious rulers decided to bring her straight to Jesus to see what He would do with her.

The law stated that she should be killed for such an offense, and they wanted to see if Jesus would uphold the law or continue to teach about mercy. What they wanted more than anything was to trick Him and make Him do something that would prove He wasn't really the Son of God.

When at last they came to where He was, the woman trembled with fear. She knew that she was guilty, and she assumed that Jesus would have her put to death because of it. She didn't dare to look at Him—she was too overcome with embarrassment.

The men threw her in front of Jesus, loudly telling the details of her sin. They reminded Him that the law said she should be stoned as punishment, and then they waited to see what He would say.

All the people around them turned their heads to look at her. She was a disgrace, and surely Jesus would agree and have her killed.

Without saying a word, Jesus lowered Himself to the ground. Everyone watched as He began to write something in the dirt with His finger.

And what did He write?

To this day, we don't know the answer, but whatever it was would change their minds, make them reconsider.

When He finished, He stood up and said to the religious rulers, "If you are standing here and have never committed a sin, by all means, pick up a stone to throw at her."

The woman was confused. Why was He talking about their sins instead of punishing her for hers?

Once more, Jesus bent down low and began to write, and as He did, people started to leave. One by one, every person who had waited for her to be killed walked away from the scene.

No stones were picked up. No stones were thrown.

Because as much as the religious leaders wanted her to be found guilty, they realized they would also have to admit that they were guilty as well. Other than Jesus, there wasn't a single person there who could say that he was perfect, which was Jesus' point exactly.

Where the law had been unbending, Christ came full of grace and love. He knew that the woman had done wrong—there was no question. But rather than agree to kill her, He reassured her that she was forgiven.

She was released from the staring, angry eyes and the hypocritical people who were more concerned about her sin than their own.

When the very last person had drifted far from them, Jesus stood alone with the woman, and He told her that she was free to go. He wasn't going to take her life as payment for her sin; He was going to give her another chance at a good and holy life.

She was speechless, dumbfounded in awe of the grace He offered.

"Go on," He said gently to the woman. "No one here condemned you, and I don't either."

Covered in mercy, she left the place where she should have died and set out to honor the One who had saved her.

—FROM JOHN 8

He

God is **merciful**, giving His forgiveness when we don't deserve it at all. Jesus has taken the ultimate punishment for our sins. So instead of the condemnation that we should receive, God gives us His grace and love in its place.

Me

We should always remember what God has done for us because when we keep it in the front of our thoughts, it reminds us how very thankful we should be to have anything good at all. He didn't leave us where we were, stuck in a pit of mistakes we could never fix on our own. Instead He reached down to us and set us above all the rubble of our own sin. If He can show us that kind of grace, who are we to do any different?

She

Lord, let Your mercy always be at the forefront of _____'s decisions and actions. Remind her of what she would have been without You, continuously keeping grace the center of her gratitude and the seed that will grow into a merciful and kind heart. When the snare of entitlement comes in and tempts her to believe she is "owed" something, give her a gentle and swift reminder of the truth: there is nothing good that comes to us that is not from Your hand (James 1:17), and it is extended to us from a place of great cost to You.

Eleos (EH lee os) is the Greek word for "mercy."
The memory verse for this story is John 8:7—
"The one without sin among you should be the first to throw a stone at her."

Alabaster

The Story of the Sinful Woman

She reached for the alabaster flask of perfume the way she had for many years, but this time she didn't smooth it onto her skin. She held it tightly in her hands, pushing the door open and running toward Simon's house without even thinking to comb her hair.

Simon and his friends wanted nothing to do with her—she knew that. She was considered the lowest of the low, and they were religious men with no time for common people. As she ran into the night, she tried not to think about what they would say to her.

"You threw your life away."

"There is nothing good that can come of someone so bad."

"You have made too many mistakes to ever be forgiven."

She had heard it all before, and she had even begun to believe it herself. But on this night, Simon had a guest who might change everything. Ignoring the chatter in her head, she turned the corner and saw his house. Just a few more steps, she told herself.

She walked into the house, following the sound of voices until she reached them. She could no longer control the tears, and as they came rushing down her face, she lowered her body to the ground by Jesus.

Memories flooded her mind, and she was overcome by the guilt she had carried for so long. She knew she had done many things wrong—there was no denying it. But this man was different, and she sensed that He might see her as more than her shadowed past. She knew how many people despised her, but she wondered something much more important: *Did God?*

As she shook with sadness, the men gathered around to see what Jesus would do. She glanced at them, silently begging them to give her a chance. When she turned to Jesus, her tears began to fall on His feet, and she bent her head lower, wiping His feet dry with her tangled hair. Wild with a broken heart, she worshipped Him by kissing His feet, ignoring anything but the purest desire to glorify Him.

In her hands was the perfume she had long used to impress men, but now she impressed it onto the feet of one man. Pressing it onto His skin as a sign of her love for Him, she continued to cry as He watched her.

While the people surrounding them whispered their disgust at her inappropriate behavior, the Lord knew what had compelled her, and it was beautiful to Him. Jesus saw the look of horror on Simon's face and immediately spoke to him.

"Simon," Jesus said, "I have something I need to say to you."

"Say it, Teacher," Simon responded.

As He often did, Jesus began to tell a parable, a story that was meant to teach people an important lesson. This story was about two men who worked for the same master. One man owed the master a very large amount of money and the other owed him a small amount. The master surprised them by telling them that neither had to pay him back and that they were both free to go. When Jesus finished, He asked Simon which of the men was probably the most grateful.

"The one who owed the most, sir," he answered.

"Yes." Jesus nodded. "And this woman understands that because she has made many, many mistakes."

There was silence.

"You, Simon, didn't even honor Me with a proper greeting."

Simon couldn't believe what he was hearing. Was Jesus actually taking the side of this filthy woman? She didn't keep any rules, and Simon had made it his life's mission to keep them. It was as if everything were upside-down to this man, Jesus.

Only it wasn't. It was exactly right. You see, both the woman and Simon were sinners, but only she realized it. It was because of her faith in God and her desperate need for His grace that she was healed.

Jesus looked at her with love, and His words erased the questions that had plagued her for so long.

"Your sins have been forgiven," He said gently. She smiled, her hair still soaked with her own sorrow.

The other people there might not have understood the power of grace, but she did.

While they stared at Him, thinking He must be a madman to forgive such a wretched woman, Jesus sent her home in peace. They were all too blinded by their own self-righteousness to see how much they needed His forgiveness too.

As she hurried home, the moon lit her path in a new way. As her fingers tightened around the flask, she thought of His words and smiled.

Forgiven. All of it forgiven.

She had poured out her heart and her perfume to the One who made all things new. And as she walked, she held her head higher than she had in years—all the while inhaling the scent of God's great mercy.

—FROM LUKE 7

He

God is **worthy** of all your praise because He alone is the King of all kings and the Lord of all lords. He deserves every wonderful thing that you can bring to His feet and so much more. You can never give God all the glory that belongs to Him no matter how hard you try; He is more wonderful than we can say and more beautiful than we can acknowledge.

Me

Make your life a constant offering of praise to the One worthy God. Don't ever let the obligations around you distract you from your main goal: to worship Him. There will be so many things that try to take our attention from Him and so many opportunities to feel like we're serving Him instead of simply being in His presence. Resist the temptation to always be "doing" things for God, and instead, make sure you are "being" with Him.

She

Lord, help _____ to be a person who is known for her extravagant love for You. Even if they don't understand it, let others be drawn to her passion and reverence for You, curious about the stillness that comes from awe. When she is tempted to be busy with things that aren't necessary, bring her back to the place You want her to be: in Your presence. Bless her with the ability to love others the way You have loved her (John 15:12).

Aphiēmi (a FEE ay me) is the Greek word for "forgive."
The memory verse for this story is Luke 7:47—
"Therefore I tell you, her many sins have been forgiven; that's why she loved much.
But the one who is forgiven little, loves little."

Two Mites

The Story of the Widow with Two Mites

Jesus and His disciples sat in the temple, watching the crowds of people come and go. Over and over, they heard the plink of coins as they fell from rich people's hands into the temple treasury. The money would be used for many different things, such as keeping the temple clean, buying incense to burn, or even to purchase the wood used during sacrifices.

Most of the people felt important when they made a big donation, and more often than not, they were so wealthy that it didn't even affect their lives. They still had plenty left over for food and clothes, so really the donation was a way to make them feel like they had given a lot to God, even though it didn't take much away from them.

As Jesus watched, a widow came along. She took two mites, which is barely a penny, and dropped them into the offering box. I wonder if the people around her started to laugh because there isn't much that can be bought with that small amount of money. But before anyone said a word, Jesus explained the truth of what she had done.

You see, the widow didn't have more money in her pockets. In fact, she didn't have any more money at home or anywhere else for that matter. Those two mites were everything she owned.

Jesus gathered His disciples and explained, "This woman has given more than every other person, because she had little, and she gave it all. The others had so much that they will hardly miss what they gave, but she doesn't even know how she will get her next meal."

The woman who had no husband to take care of her and no way to know how she would even stay alive was willing to give everything she had to God because she believed in Him that much. Her faith was amazing, and there's no question that she was rewarded in heaven for the way she trusted the Lord.

179

God isn't really worried about how much we give to Him. After all, He can do anything, with or without our money. But He does care about our hearts and why we give. The widow is a wonderful example to us because she was willing to sacrifice her comfort and her security in order to bless God.

God never laughs at us when we feel like we don't have much to offer; in fact He loves to use what we give Him and turn it into something beautiful. As the coins fall one after another, deep into the treasury, God isn't counting the money.

He's counting the cost to us instead.

If we leave with empty pockets, we are making room for God to work and to show us how He can take care of us. Trusting Him that much isn't easy, and it won't always be fun. But just like the widow who brought two mites, we are inviting Him to bless us more than money ever could.

—FROM LUKE 21

He

God is **transcendent**, which means He is above all of creation. He doesn't need anything in the universe to keep Him going because His existence is totally separate from ours. He chooses to come near to us and enter into relationship with us, but it isn't because He has to. He would be perfectly fine on His own, but He chooses to be near to us.

Me

God gives us good gifts—not so we can store them up and pile them away, but so we can use them to teach more people about His love and kindness. When we're selfish, refusing to be generous, it means we have forgotten that everything belongs to Him. When we act on that belief, even when it means giving up the very little we might have, we show our true devotion and obedience to the God who let it be in our hands in the first place.

She

Lord, make _____ a girl who lives with her hands open, refusing to tighten her grip on the things You have allowed her to have. Keep her from believing she has any more right to good gifts than anyone else, and cultivate in her a true desire to be kind and generous to others (Ephesians 4:32) out of her genuine recognition of ownership. None of it is ours, Lord, and the moment we believe differently, we have put ourselves in a precarious position where we become numb to the importance of stewardship. Let me always teach her how to give her life away for the sake of the One who did so for me.

__Dōron__ (DOH ron) is the Greek word for "offering."
The memory verse for this story is Luke 21:3—
"I tell you the truth," He said. "This poor widow has put in more than all of them."

The One Thing

The Story of Mary and Martha and the Dinner

$\mathcal{M}$artha rushed around the house to make sure everything was in place for her dinner guest. Even though she had been preparing for hours, it still seemed like it wasn't quite perfect. The table was set, and the food was almost ready, but she couldn't bear to sit down. As Martha paced, Mary peered out the window to see if she could spot them yet.

"Martha, rest. It's wonderful," Mary whispered. But Martha just shook her head, smoothed her apron again, and headed into the kitchen with a heavy sigh.

When the knock finally came, Martha rushed out in front of Mary to open the door, welcoming the group into her home and motioning to their chairs at the table.

As the dinner plates clanged on the table and laughter filled the room, Mary sat at the feet of Jesus and listened to Him teach. Martha, on the other hand, was busying herself with pouring water and cleaning silverware. Back and forth she went, gathering empty dishes and making sure everyone had plenty to eat.

After this had gone on for some time, Martha became frustrated at the way her sister Mary was lazily sitting on the ground while Martha was busy working.

"Jesus," Martha said, "don't You care that my sister has left me to do all this work alone?" Her voice was as sharp as a knife, and she wanted Him to do something about the situation.

"Tell her that she needs to help instead of just sitting there!" she finished, her face sweaty with effort and anger.

She looked from Jesus to Mary and then back again, anxious for Him to set Mary straight. Jesus smiled gently at Martha, but His words were not at all what she was expecting to hear.

"Martha, Martha," He said softly, "you are so worried about getting all of these things done that you've missed the one thing that's the most important."

Martha squinted her eyes, confused at His reply.

Before she could say another word, Jesus continued.

"Mary has chosen correctly, and she will continue to do what she is doing," Jesus explained.

This was shocking to Martha, who had been sure that all of her work would show Christ that she loved Him the most. After all, she was the one who had served Him, not Mary. She had made sure that the meal was perfectly presented and that everyone had plenty of delicious food. She had cleared the plates, refilled the drinks, and had barely sat down herself—and now Jesus was complimenting Mary instead?

But the truth was that Mary recognized how amazing it was to be in the presence of Jesus, and she couldn't imagine doing any of the other tasks when she could simply soak up His wisdom. Her heart was filled to the brim as she worshipped the Lord, and she knew that all the other duties could wait.

Jesus loved both Mary and Martha dearly, but His words taught Martha a valuable lesson about the way Christ wants us to worship.

Never let yourself be so caught up in all the presentations that you miss being present with Him.

—FROM LUKE 10

He

God is **jealous** in His love for us. Usually when you hear the word **jealous**, it means someone wants something that another person has. In a way, that's what it means for God too. However, He doesn't want our things or our abilities—He wants all of our love. He doesn't want to share our love for Him with other things like money, fame, or food. He wants our love to be entirely focused on Him and not given away to lesser things. He is a jealous God because He cannot stand to see us waste our devotion on anything less than Himself.

Me

Do you respect God? Do you respect other people? When your mother or father asks you to do something, do you obey or disobey? When you don't have any respect for people and you ignore their guidance, you are rebelling against God Himself. He has placed people in our lives to take care of us, and part of taking care of us is teaching us what is right and what is wrong. Be quick to respond to your leaders with a kind and honoring tone, and in your respect for them, you will show your respect for God.

She

Lord, help _____ to be a God-honoring and respectful child who turns away from idols and toward the one true God (1 Corinthians 8:5–6). When she is tempted to respond with a rebellious spirit, pushing her boundaries and alienating those who lead her, keep Your model of humility close in her thoughts. As I lead her, help me do so in ways that keep her eternal goals in mind, taking care not to nag at her or frustrate her unnecessarily. Help me identify the areas where I need to give her room to grow in You instead of pushing my agenda, and lead her into the kind of relationship with You that makes her question anything that stands in the way of pure devotion to You.

Proskuneō (pros koo NE oh) is the Greek word for "worship."
The memory verse for this story is Luke 10:41–42—
"Martha, Martha, you are worried and upset about many things,
but one thing is necessary."

Four Days

The Story of Mary and Martha and the Death of Lazarus

$\mathcal{B}$ecause Mary and Martha were Jesus' dear friends, they assumed that He would come running back to town as soon as He got their message.

"Our brother Lazarus, whom You love, is sick."

They knew how much Jesus cared for Lazarus, and they knew that He could heal him. So they waited. And waited. And waited.

While they waited, Lazarus got sicker and sicker until finally he died. Mary and Martha were shocked that the Lord hadn't come to them or even sent word to them.

Four days after Lazarus had died, the sisters heard that Jesus was on His way. Mary stayed behind in the house, but Martha stood and ran to meet Him.

When she finally saw the Lord, she cried, asking Him why He hadn't come sooner. "If You had been here," Martha sobbed, "my brother would still be alive!"

Jesus looked at her kindly, and said, "Your brother will rise again."

Martha didn't understand what He meant. She thought Jesus was talking about Lazarus being alive in heaven, but actually, He wasn't.

Martha ran to the house where Mary was waiting and shouted, "He's here! He has asked you to come and see Him!" Mary immediately rushed out of the house, running until at last she reached Jesus on the edge of town.

Falling at His feet, she cried just as her sister had and told Jesus she believed Lazarus would still be alive if He had come sooner.

Jesus knew what was going to happen, and He knew that they would be happy about it. But He also knew that they couldn't see it yet and that their hearts were breaking with sadness.

He asked them to bring Him to the tomb where Lazarus had been buried. Even though good was coming, Jesus loved them so much that He felt their sorrow like it was His own. He cried with them as they walked to the tomb.

When they reached the cave where Lazarus was, Jesus asked Martha to move the large stone that was blocking the entrance. Martha hesitated.

"Lord, Lazarus has been dead for four days. If I move this stone, the smell will be terrible," she said.

Jesus spoke to her, reminding her that if she believed, she would see the glory of God. Martha trusted Jesus, so she walked forward and used all of her strength to roll away the huge stone.

After she had done this, Jesus prayed to His Father God. He thanked Him for what He was about to do.

Mary and Martha watched, wondering what was going to happen next.

"Lazarus," Jesus shouted into the cave, "come out!"

There were many people there now, gathered around to see what Jesus was going to do there. They didn't really believe He was the Son of God, and they were curious about His power.

There was silence for a moment as all of their eyes looked into the dark cave.

And then they saw something that they thought was impossible.

Lazarus, still wrapped up in his grave clothes, walked out of the tomb alive.

"Unwrap him," Jesus commanded, "and let him go."

Suddenly there were shouts of amazement and tears of joy, and there were also many people who were suspicious of Jesus. After all, who can bring the dead back to life? They wondered if it was a trick or some kind of strange illusion, and they ran to the people in charge to tell them what had happened.

The leaders did not take this news very well because it meant that someone could actually be more powerful than they were. That was the last thing they wanted.

So the leaders made a plan right then and there: Jesus must be stopped at all costs. They would have Him murdered before anyone else could believe in Him.

Jesus had known that coming back to Bethlehem was dangerous, and He knew that the rulers' anger would lead to something awful. But just as He had with Mary and Martha, He saw something they couldn't.

Even in the sadness, Jesus knew there was a greater happiness coming. His days on earth were coming to a close, but that wasn't going to be the end of the story.

Not even death can keep God from those He loves. In fact, sometimes it just makes a way for us to believe so that we can see the miracle for ourselves.

—FROM JOHN 11

He

Even in the times when it doesn't seem like it to us, God is **good**. He is good all the time, in every way, and He always will be. Oftentimes we don't understand how He can let something happen to us that seems bad, but He promises us that He will use even that terrible thing for good. He is the ultimate Redeemer, able to make beauty from ashes.

Me

Part of what should make us look different to the world is the way we have compassion for other people. That means we pay attention to the way they might be feeling, and we care about ways we could bring God's bright love to their darkness. If you just go around looking out for yourself, you're going to miss the amazing gifts Jesus has offered you. You aren't the only person who matters to God, and it's important that you remember you are one of many in a great big family of children. We have to look out for each other, taking care of one another and loving well in just the same way that Jesus did.

She

Lord, give _____ the gift of Your compassion, making her well aware of the needs, sadness, and desperation of the people who don't know You. Give her eyes to see the poor as her brothers and sisters, not inferior to her but needing her resources and prayer. Don't allow this world to give her a jaded view of Your heart for us, because we know that in all things You are working good (Romans 8:28). Even when we don't see it, we can be confident that the seed is simply growing in the soil of our circumstances, sure to produce a beautiful harvest one day.

Anastasi (an AHS tas is) is the Greek work for "resurrection."
The memory verse for this story is John 11:25—
"I am the resurrection and the life. The one who believes in Me, even if he dies, will live."

191

Beautiful

The Story of Mary of Bethany

*M*ary and Martha were still in awe of the way Jesus had brought their brother back to life, and they gathered up a group of people to come to a dinner to honor Him. The guests were all people who had followed Jesus, but there was one man there who was going to betray Him.

As Martha made the food, everyone sat around the table and talked. Lazarus was relaxing there as well, when suddenly Mary came into the room with a large bottle of perfume. She wanted Jesus to know how much she loved Him and how little she loved the things that seemed important to the world.

She knew the perfume was worth a lot of money, but money didn't matter. He mattered.

In order to show her devotion to the Lord, she wiped the perfume on His feet and ran her hair through it. The entire house began to smell like beautiful perfume, and everyone was happy except for one person.

Judas shouted in anger, "Why would you waste that perfume this way? You could have sold it for a lot of money! You could have used that money to feed the poor!"

Judas actually didn't care about the poor at all, but he did care about himself. He took care of the moneybag for Jesus, and he imagined what he could have done with the money if the perfume had been sold instead of poured on Jesus' feet. His heart was wicked and jealous, and he had no idea what really loving God looked like.

He waited for Jesus to yell at Mary, but when the Lord spoke, it silenced him.

"Leave her alone," He said.

The joyful sounds of a celebration stopped, and everyone looked up to see what Jesus would do next.

They all knew that a pound of perfume was worth a year's salary, and that money could have been used in other ways. But they wanted to know what Jesus thought about it, and as Judas Iscariot squinted his eyes in anger, Jesus spoke again.

"You aren't going to have Me forever, you know," He said. "In fact, I'm going to die soon, and this perfume will prepare My body for death." The guests looked at one another in confusion.

Mary didn't realize what was going to happen to Jesus in the coming days; she just wanted to show Him that she honored Him. But now, as He spoke, she became sad thinking about the days when He would no longer be with them.

"What Mary has done for Me is beautiful," He finished, explaining that there would always be poor people to care for, but His time on earth was nearly over.

Judas was furious, and he decided he would get revenge. He was one of the twelve men who had been traveling with Jesus for years, but his stubborn heart refused to worship Him the way Mary had.

As soon as he had the opportunity, Judas snuck away to meet with the chief priests. He knew they had been looking for Jesus in order to have Him arrested, and he asked them what his reward would be if he revealed the Lord's location.

"Thirty denarii," they told him, eager to get their hands on the man causing all the commotion in Jerusalem.

Judas nodded in response, explaining that he would betray Jesus.

When the moon came up and they were together again for a dinner, Jesus told the disciples that one of them was going to betray Him. They all shook their heads and denied it, but Jesus insisted. Judas knew he was the one who would turn Him in, and he waited for the perfect moment.

Jesus, knowing it was nearly time for His death, went to the garden of Gethsemane to pray. After some time passed, Jesus told the disciples with Him that His betrayer was coming, and sure enough, there was Judas, walking toward Him with a crowd of people. Judas had told the chief priests that he would kiss Jesus' hand, and that's how they would know it was Him.

As Judas kissed His hand, Jesus whispered, "Friend, do what you came to do." Jesus knew Judas would betray Him, and He knew it would lead to His death.

Mary, the one who loved Jesus more than anything, was willing to pour out her most valuable possessions to worship Him. Judas on the other hand, for the payment of thirty denarii, betrayed the Son of God with a kiss, showing that he never really loved Him at all.

On that dark night, the followers of Jesus scattered in fear as the soldiers took Him away. As Jesus was carried into the darkness, the scent of worship all around Him, He knew what was about to happen.

With His heart pounding in His chest, Jesus the promised Christ walked into His destiny as the Savior of the world.

—FROM JOHN 12

He

The Bible says that God is "**holy, holy, holy**" (Isaiah 6:3), and it's the only characteristic of God that is repeated three times. That means it is the most important thing about Him: He is holy. He is pure, perfect, good, and just in all things, and the fact that He is the only being who can do this exactly right makes Him holy. It sets Him apart from any created being, and even though it is possible (and important) for us to try to be holy like Him, we will never, ever be as wonderful as He is.

Me

The only way we can appropriately respond to the holiness of God is to offer Him our total devotion, focusing our lives on honoring and serving Him. When you are a worshipful person, it means you are quick and steady with your praise of God and you don't put anyone in front of Him. Your whole life is a song being played for the King of all kings. Make every note count!

She

Lord, give_____ a sense of Your utter holiness, allowing her to tremble in Your presence in recognition of who You are and what You have chosen to do for her. Let her never move so far away from her genuine and good fear of You (Psalm 19:9) that she starts to believe she can do it on her own. We know what comes from moving away from You, and my desire is for her to be so committed to Your laws and Your ways that she can't imagine living anywhere but in the presence of the holy God.

Aleiphō (al AY fo) is the Greek word for "anoint."
The memory verse for this story is John 12:3—
"Then Mary took a pound of fragrant oil—pure and expensive nard—anointed Jesus' feet,
and wiped His feet with her hair."

James and John had been telling their mother Salome about Jesus for years. They had been His followers since the beginning, and now it had come to the hardest day in His life.

She wanted to be there, even though she didn't.

She wanted to show Him that she cared for Him, even though she knew it would break her heart.

She wanted to believe that He was going to find a way around the terrible punishment given to Him by Pontius Pilate, but as the crowd gathered, she knew it was too late.

"Here He comes!" a voice cried out.

There was Jesus, climbing the tall hill while carrying a wooden cross on His back. Another man, Simon, was helping Him with the weight of the cross, which had become too heavy for His tired body. Jesus was covered with cuts and bruises, and His eyes were red with pain. Salome was overcome with sadness, her hands covering her mouth in horror as she watched the soldiers kick Him and laugh.

His clothes had been torn off of Him and given away piece by piece, all except His tunic, which was left in one piece. Resting on His head and piercing His skin was a crown made of thorns, and above Him a sign read, "King of the Jews." That was their way of making fun of Him and calling Him a liar.

How dare He say that He was the Son of God! The Jews had been waiting for a redeemer, but they didn't believe Jesus was that man. They imagined that He would come in great power—maybe as a king or a warrior—but this man? Born in a manger and a friend to the lowest of the low?

It couldn't be.

Cross

The Story of Salome at the Cross

So they raised His cross up high, His arms and legs nailed in place. They shouted at Him and called Him weak, saying, "If You were God, You would save Yourself." To them, He was just a person pretending to be God.

But Salome, Mary of Magdalene, and Mary (the Lord's mother) stood in the shadows of the cross, and they cried because they knew that He was exactly who He said He was.

Two men hung on either side of Jesus, each one being crucified for stealing. One of the men saw Jesus and knew He was God. He put his faith in Jesus right then and there as he hung on a cross about to die. And it wasn't too late for him. Jesus told the man that He would see him in heaven that day, all because he had chosen to believe.

Jesus looked at the people gathered below Him, spitting on Him and shouting for Him to die. In His great empathy and caring for the whole world, He shouted, "Father, forgive them. They don't know what they're doing!"

Since the day He came into the world, Jesus had been love. He welcomed the people everyone else ignored, and He healed the people everyone else saw as useless. He had willingly allowed all of this to unfold for exactly this moment, when He would make everything right again.

A scream, loud and shrill, exploded from beside her, and Salome looked to see Mary the mother of Christ lying on her face in agony. She could hardly bear to see her son being tortured and killed.

It went on like this for hours, and the crowds simply watched and waited to see what this man would do. After some time, Jesus asked for a drink, so some of the men put a sponge on a tall stick and lifted it to His mouth so He could drink the sour wine.

That was the last request He would make during this life on earth. A few moments later, His words came like daggers to those who loved Him.

"It is finished."

With that, Jesus took one last breath of our sin-soaked world, and He closed His eyes. The curtain in the temple ripped in half as He died, and the stones around Him split while the ground trembled. The soldiers were amazed and shook their heads as they began to wonder if He really had been the Christ.

There, on a hill high above the world, Jesus the promised One gave Himself up in exchange for us. No more would we be separated from God by sin because His sacrifice gave us another chance.

"The King of the Jews?" they had sneered, laughing at His claims.

Indeed, He was.

The Chosen One. The Messiah. The Promise. The Redeemer.

After all these years, their King had finally come.

But instead of worshipping Him, they nailed Him to a cross and set Him high above them to die. And while His blood trickled down His legs, His face, and the tall wooden cross, they turned their heads and refused His gift of grace.

His body was lowered later that day and given to a loyal follower named Joseph. Tenderly, Joseph wrapped Jesus' body in linen and then set Him inside a tomb that had been carved out of a rock. To protect Jesus, Joseph rolled a large, heavy stone in front of the opening of the tomb.

When Joseph finished, he walked away, and it's likely he didn't realize that death and stones are no match for the living God. Soon, though, he would see it for himself.

There, behind a huge rock in the dark of a cave, God was preparing the greatest miracle of all time.

—FROM MATTHEW 27; MARK 15; LUKE 23; JOHN 19

He

In all the trials and tribulations we face in this life, we can rely on God to be our **Comforter**. Many times, He doesn't change things to be the way we want them to be, but He does offer Himself as a kind and loving friend. He keeps our tears in a bottle (Psalm 56:8), and one day they will be no more (Revelation 21:4). In the meantime, you can be certain of His constant and genuine affection for you and His offer to carry you through the darkest nights of sadness.

Me

Being faithful to God means that you keep loving Him, obeying Him, and trusting Him no matter what you feel or experience. It is the commitment to keeping our eyes on Him, even in the times when He seems far away or small. Being a faithful servant to God means you don't let your circumstances convince you that He is any different; you just keep looking to Him even when you can't see Him, and eventually, you will!

She

Lord, bless _____ with the desire to be faithful to You in all her ways. Give her a heart that seeks Your goodness above the world's pleasure, and the unmistakable conviction that comes to wrestle the blessings away from the Gift-giver (Genesis 32:36). You bless us so graciously with comfort when we are broken (2 Corinthians 1:3–5); make it the goal of our days to remain in You so we never miss a second of Your goodness.

Parakaleō (par ak al EH oh) is the Greek word for "comfort."
The memory verse for this story is Luke 24:2–3—
"They found the stone rolled away from the tomb. They went in but did not find the body of the Lord Jesus."

Alive

*The Story of Mary the Magdalene
and the Resurrection*

When Mary from the town of Magdalene met Jesus, she was suffering from something terrible: she was possessed by seven demons. Jesus healed her, calling the evil out of her body, and she had been a loyal follower ever since.

In all the days that she walked with Him, she was in awe of the way He loved people. She had seen Him performing miracles and teaching those around Him, and she wanted to be true to Him for her entire life.

She had been in the crowd on the day that the darkness filled the sky, and she cried as she saw her precious Savior dying on the cross. Alongside her friends and other followers of Jesus, she was devastated by His death. She was devastated to have lost the One who meant so much to her, and she couldn't imagine living her days without Him.

Before the sun had come up the next day, she was hurrying to His tomb to finish preparing His body for burial. She wasn't strong enough to move the stone, and she wasn't sure what she would do when she got there. When at last she reached the tomb, her blood ran cold.

The stone was gone.

She and the other women who had traveled with her peered into the tomb and were shocked to see someone dressed in white and seated inside.

"Don't be afraid," he responded. "Jesus isn't here anymore."

It was clear that He was gone, and the women didn't know what to do. Their beloved Jesus must have been stolen in the night, and now all that remained were His grave clothes, folded and set aside.

"He has risen," the angel explained, "just as He told you He would."

But they didn't know what to believe. They thought they should tell the disciples what had happened, so they ran away to find them. Later, Mary was weeping outside the tomb, still grieving the death of Jesus, and she heard a voice speaking gently.

"Woman," the voice said, "why are you crying?"

"Because they've taken my Lord," she sobbed, "and I don't know where they've put Him." Turning her head, she saw a man that she didn't recognize.

He asked her why she was so upset, and because she thought he was a gardener, she begged for him to tell her where the body of Christ had been taken.

"Mary," she heard. But this time, she recognized the voice.

It wasn't another angel, and it wasn't a gardener as she first thought.

It was Jesus, alive and well.

"Teacher!" she shouted, standing to her feet and rushing toward Him.

After all the days and nights and all the promises and power, this was what they had waited for. He stood in front of her, His hands and feet still wounded but His lungs and limbs full of life.

There was no other explanation—this man was the promised One.

"Go and tell the others," He whispered. And before she could think, she forced her feet, one in front of the other as she stumbled to get her balance to run. It was true; it was all true.

She had been devastated by His death, but all along He had known that this was the next part of the plan. He had to go through such a dark and terrible ordeal in order to get to this, where three days had passed and everyone thought He was gone forever.

When the earth shook and everything seemed undone, the Lamb of God was preparing to return. And three days after His death, He did exactly that.

All the armies and disbelief in the world couldn't stop Him, and to this day they still haven't. We don't get to see Him the way that Mary did, with her eyes wide and her heart pounding, but we do still encounter the risen Lord.

And when we believe in Him, we tell Him so. We receive the same amazing gift as the robber on the cross beside Him: forever life with God in heaven, the likes of which we cannot begin to comprehend.

—FROM MARK 16; LUKE 24; JOHN 20

He

God is **omniscient**, which means that He knows all things. ALL things. There isn't a single, teensy-tiny, itsy-bitsy thing that escapes His notice. Of course, our brains can't imagine knowing that much, but it's just part of who He is.

Me

When you say you are sorry, but you don't change the way you did things, you aren't really sorry. Being repentant means that you understand where you were wrong, you have confessed it, and you have moved in a different direction. For example, if you apologize for hitting your sister, but then you do it again a few minutes later, you weren't really repentant. The way someone knows you are truly sorry is by changed behavior in response to the realization that you were wrong. That's true for God too. He doesn't just want you to say you're sorry about things; He wants you to show you are by changing.

She

When life seems barren and hopeless, and death seems to have had the final say, bring this story to _____'s mind, and let her bask in the light of Your faithfulness to her, replacing the grave with breath and the end with a new beginning. It would be easy to feel the sting of life and believe You have given up or turned away from us, but instead we cling to Your promises and we claim Your goodness for ourselves, confidently moving forward in ways that show You we want to honor and bless You. Let her be quick to repent, convinced of the importance of humbling herself before You (1 Peter 5:6–7).

Metanoeō (met an oh EH oh) is the Greek word for "repent."
The memory verse for this story is John 20:18—
"I have seen the Lord!"

The Price

The Story of Sapphira

After Christ returned to heaven, all His believers decided the best thing they could do was band together and make sure everyone was taken care of. Instead of worrying about building up their own houses and fortunes, they gave everything they had to make sure that everyone had enough. That way, the poor people weren't poor anymore, and the rich people weren't just keeping all of their money to themselves. They were like one big family that looked out for one another.

Ananias and his wife, Sapphira, were part of this group, and they pretended that they were doing their part, but actually they were being very sneaky and selfish.

They sold their property and got a large amount of money for it, but then they decided to keep some of it for themselves instead of turning it all over to the group. There wasn't a rule about giving all of their money to the group, but they thought that if they could make it look like they were, people would be very impressed with them.

"They'll never know," Ananias said, "and they'll think we are the most generous of anybody."

"You're right," Sapphira agreed. "That way we will have some money left for ourselves too."

"Let's just tell them we sold it for less. Then they'll think we are giving them everything," Ananias said.

Sapphira agreed, and the plan was hatched. After hiding the extra money, Ananias took the rest to Peter and laid it at his feet, expecting quite a fuss to be made about how kind he and Sapphira were to give everything.

But Peter knew that something was wrong, and he asked Ananias how much he had sold his property for. Ananias, not wanting to look bad, told Peter that this was all the money he had received.

And that's where he made his worst mistake. He could have confessed that he and Sapphira had kept some of the money at home, but he didn't. He lied right to Peter's face, and Peter knew it.

"You aren't just lying to us, Ananias. You're lying to God," Peter said.

As soon as Ananias heard those words, he fell down dead on the ground. The people around him covered up his body and then buried him, knowing that God had punished him for his deceit.

Three hours later, and with no idea what had happened to her husband, Sapphira showed up at the same place. Peter asked her the same question that he had asked Ananias, and the people watching held their breath waiting to see what she would say.

"Peter, we've given you all the money from the sale," Sapphira said without hesitating.

"Your husband told us that lie, and now he is dead and buried. Because you decided to do the same, the same thing will happen to you," Peter explained.

Sapphira stared at him, confused. She never thought she would be caught.

"The men who buried Ananias are waiting right outside that door, and they are going to bury you as well," Peter finished, sad that she hadn't chosen the truth.

At that very moment, Sapphira took her last breath and fell to the floor. She was a victim of her own awful choice. She was focused on making everyone believe she was kind and thoughtful, and she thought that by spinning her stories, she could convince them.

But she underestimated God's power and His desire for goodness in His followers. If only Sapphira had been more concerned with her heart than her appearances, she might have lived a long and wonderful life. Instead, she pretended her way right into the ground, never even having the chance to spend the money that buried her there.

—FROM ACTS 5

He

God is **righteous**, which means that He knows what is ultimately right and what is ultimately wrong because His very nature is the standard of what is right. That's why He is unaffected by outside influences that don't really matter. He isn't tricked by a smooth talker, and He isn't turned away by a brokenhearted cry. He sees everything through pure eyes, unfiltered by the details of this world.

Me

We might not get all of the things we want in this life, and that's going to be hard to deal with. What we have to remember is that we might think something is best for us when really it isn't, and God is acting on our behalf to determine that. Instead of always looking at what other people have, or wishing your way into jealousy, practice being content with what you have and grateful for everything He allows.

She

Cultivate a heart of contentment (Philippians 4:11) in _____, leading her to trust Your provision instead of spending her hours in envious, doubtful, or fearful thoughts. You are fully able to provide for us, and what You have given us is enough. Help her embrace the freedom that comes from learning to be content in all situations, relying on nothing in this world to satisfy her the way You can.

Autarkēs (aw TAR case) is the Greek word for "content."
The memory verse for this story is Acts 5:9—
"Why did you agree to test the Spirit of the Lord?"

216

Another Breath

The Story of Tabitha

She wasn't well-known because she was extraordinarily beautiful or wealthy, but Tabitha was one of the most treasured women in Joppa. She was always eager to serve, and her kindness and laughter could fill any space with joy.

Her passion was to care for the poor, and because she was an amazing seamstress, she spent her days sewing clothes for all the people who couldn't afford to buy them. She had been a follower of Jesus and had decided to give her life to whatever would make His more famous. She didn't mind that it was a small job, and she wasn't worried about getting credit for doing it. She just wanted to honor the Lord.

Unexpectedly, Tabitha became ill and passed away in her home. When her neighbors found her there, they were desperately sad and called for help.

"Peter is in a town nearby!" they shouted. "Let's call for him and see if there's anything he can do!"

As soon as Peter heard what had happened, he rushed to Joppa and climbed the stairs to where Tabitha's body lay.

One by one, the women walked up to him, explaining how much she had done and how much she would be missed. They clung to the clothes she had been sewing, holding them out for Peter to see.

"All she did was sew," they explained, "and she gave her whole heart to those who had less than she did."

Tears covered their cheeks as they told him stories about her, and Peter was equally upset to have lost such a kind and selfless sister in Christ.

"Leave, please," Peter whispered, pointing to the door as his face crumpled in sadness. The women left, their sobs echoing as they closed the door behind them.

There, in the simple room, Peter knelt by Tabitha and prayed to God. He was so troubled by her death, and he begged God to help him.

Finally, after a few moments, he spoke quietly but with confidence.

"Tabitha, get up."

As soon as the words left his mouth, her eyelids began to move and then opened. Her mouth inhaled one breath after another as she looked at Peter, trying to understand what was happening.

He reached for her and helped her to stand up on her feet, and then he called for her friends to come. One by one, they entered the room to see her standing beside Peter, completely healed.

They shouted and jumped and praised God for the miracle, and then they rushed to tell all the others what had happened.

Tabitha's life had been devoted to God, and her hands had been working hard to take care of His children. Everything she had, she had given away.

And when her time on this earth came to an end, the Lord brought her back in a way that only He could.

After that day, Tabitha did become famous, but not because she had done anything amazing. No, in fact, she hadn't done anything at all. But rather, God had shown His power in her because she was so willing to be His.

Many people put their faith in Christ because of her story, and nothing could have made her more joyful. After all, she had been given another chance to sew for her brothers and sisters, and it seemed that more and more were being added every day.

As her needles danced and her story traveled far and wide, Tabitha lived every moment in thankfulness. It was her honor to sew for those who had nothing, because really, she knew the truth.

She was, and had always been, sewing a beautiful offering for the God who had given her everything.

—FROM ACTS 9

He

There is **only One God**, and don't let anyone tell you any different. Many people look to other gods, claiming that they are as big and powerful as God, but it's a lie meant to distract us from Him.

Me

God wants us to extend His love to others by taking care of the people who aren't able to take good care of themselves. We are told to take care of the poor, giving them help and prayer because they need it desperately. Pray about the ways that God might use you to bless someone in need, and be faithful to follow through with helping as a sign of your faith in God.

She

Lord, give _____ a heart for the poor of the world, and show her the ways You have called her to alleviate that condition for Your sake and through Your power. You have not given us wealth so that we may rest in our riches (Proverbs 21:13) but rather so that we can run to offer it to those less fortunate. Help me to show her the great need in the world and to inspire her to be a part of the answer to that need.

Epieikēs (ep ee i CASE) is the Greek word for "gentle."
The memory verse for this story is Acts 9:36—
"She was always doing good works and acts of charity."

Purple Cloth

The Story of Lydia

As Lydia walked along the river, she heard a commotion ahead of her. "He'll be here soon!" they exclaimed.

A man named Paul was coming to their town to tell them his story. Everyone had heard stories of Jesus, and they were eager to hear about Him from one of His own apostles.

Lydia was a well-respected and successful businesswoman who was known for the beautiful purple fabric she sold in the market. She found her friends there and sat with them for a little while, discussing their work and their families. While they sat, Paul came along, and all the people turned to listen to him. It wasn't long before they were captivated by his words.

"I didn't believe in Him at first," he explained, trying to make eye contact with each of the people there. "In fact, I persecuted people who did believe, because I was so opposed to Him."

They leaned in closer, amazed at what he was saying.

"When the very first person was killed for being a follower of Christ, I was in the crowd. I cheered them on and celebrated his death." Paul paused. "They used to call me Saul back then."

Lydia looked around her, curious what other people thought of his stories.

"As I traveled along the road one day, I heard the voice of the Lord Jesus Christ. He spoke to me and asked me why I was doing terrible things to His people," Paul said. "And then I saw a bright light that blinded me for several days."

Nobody moved, because they could sense the power in Paul's words.

"But Jesus sent one of His followers to me, and that man restored my sight." Paul shook his head, still amazed. "Jesus is the Son of God, just as He said He was."

Lydia listened to his words, and as she did, the Lord moved her to believe. She knew in her heart that what Paul was saying was true, and she told everyone that she wanted to become a Christ follower, or a "Christian," as well.

Paul rejoiced over her faith, and he baptized her in front of the crowd as a sign of her new life with Jesus.

Lydia's entire family also came to believe in Christ, and they were baptized that very same day. She decided that from then on, her house would be open to anyone who wanted to learn more about Jesus.

"Please, come stay at my house!" she urged Paul, inviting him to tell them even more about Jesus.

Paul was very grateful to have a nice, warm bed to sleep in, and Lydia loved having Paul there in her house where she could hear him talk about his ministry. But not long after he came to stay, he had to leave again to tell more people about the Lord.

Although she was sad to see him go, Lydia forced her best smile as she hugged him good-bye. "If you ever come this way again, you are always welcome here. Always."

"Thank you," Paul said. "I'm so glad to have met you. And I'll always remember you because you were the very first person I baptized in this part of the world."

Lydia didn't know that Paul would, in fact, be back to stay with her one day, but it would be under very different circumstances. People would be angry that he was teaching about Jesus, and eventually Paul would be put in jail and tortured because of what he claimed. During that last stay in Lydia's home, he would encourage her to keep her faith strong and her heart tender for the Lord.

And then she would hug him one last time before the news came that he had been killed for his beliefs. At one time, he had been an enemy of Christ because of his hatred of Christ, but in the end, Paul would die because of his deep love for Him.

Even though Lydia cried when she heard the news, she knew that it wouldn't be forever. Because of their faith in Jesus, Lydia would see Paul again in heaven. Until then, she would keep sharing the same message he had brought to the riverside, knowing it had the power to change lives the same way it had changed both of theirs.

—FROM ACTS 16

He

God is **eternal**; He has no beginning, and He will never end. He always was and always will be. He didn't show up at some point, and He won't ever die. It's hard for us to imagine that because we are used to things starting and ending, but God is different.

Me

When you are a person who works hard, you're called industrious. Industrious people look for ways to keep working instead of being lazy, and they want to make sure they aren't just wasting precious time. Think about the ways you use your time. Are they things that will matter in heaven, or are they just things that keep you busy now? Focus on doing things that bring God the attention and praise He deserves so that you don't choose the easiest thing instead of the best thing.

She

Lord, give _____ a tenacious and willing spirit to work for You, eagerly searching for what is the best use of her time. When her friends are lost in video games and gossip, raise her up to be an example of pure devotion. Let her passion be for You and let the work of her hands be a natural overflow of that love, giving those around her a beautiful picture of time well spent (Titus 2:7–8).

Aiōnios (ahee OH nee os) is the Greek word for "eternal."
The memory verse for this story is Acts 16:14—
"The Lord opened her heart to pay attention to what was spoken by Paul."

Speak

The Story of Priscilla

$\mathcal{N}$o matter where she went in life, she wanted to be by her husband's side.

"Priscilla!" Aquila called, and she grabbed her things to meet him outside. They had been expecting their dear friend Paul to come and visit, and he was finally here.

"Come in, come in!" she urged with a smile, pouring a glass of cold water for him to drink.

Aquila embraced Paul and then invited him inside the house. "Yes, by all means, Paul. Come in and tell us about your travels."

Paul's shoulders settled, and he took a deep breath. He was so relieved to be with others who loved the Lord, and he felt like he could relax with them and be honest about how difficult it had been.

Priscilla came and sat with them, offering Paul a kind smile and a plate of fresh-baked bread. She smiled at Aquila, nodding for him to take some as well.

Paul spoke softly, his voice shaking with emotion.

"It's been horrific," he said. "But I know it's right, and I'll keep going. Everyone I reach with the truth is worth it."

For hours they listened as Paul recounted stories of prison and the fear that often came alongside his journeys. They shook their heads and prayed for him, honored to be able to spend time with a man who loved God so much.

When Priscilla and Aquila said good-bye to Paul, they knew it was possible they would never see him again because he lived a dangerous life. They always hugged him like it was the last time, just in case it was.

When he left, they were even more determined to spend their days teaching about Christ, and their courage soared after hearing his amazing stories. Priscilla and Aquila were a team, and they wanted their lives to be a beautiful picture of Christ's extravagant love. Everywhere they went, they went together, preaching the name of Jesus and building each other up.

Priscilla and Aquila traveled long distances hand in hand, always eager to see what God had next for them. Even though they were exhausted by the end of every day, they always went to bed excited about what might happen next because they knew that the Lord was guiding their steps.

When we look back at Adam and Eve and the mistake they made, it might seem as if everything had gone wrong with the world. Because of what they started, our lives should have ended.

I wonder if Priscilla ever thought about the garden from so many years ago or the way Eve had chosen her own heart over God's. I imagine she did; I also imagine it made Priscilla even more grateful for the fruit that came from her ministry.

And every single day, as Priscilla walked with her arm looped through Aquila's, she would smile because she knew what God had given them.

Another chance.

After all, the great King had made a way for us, even as we stumbled out of Eden. It was a long and difficult road, the hardest of which was reserved for Jesus to bear. But after He did, well . . .

Everything changed.

All those who believe in Him have heaven to look forward to and, in the meantime, a clear and steady path that simply follows Him. Everything we do, everywhere we go, and everyone we meet—they all give us chances to do exactly as Priscilla did.

We walk tall because we know who our Father is, and we smile when we hear His name.

Jesus.

The man who came to make us daughters—to make us *whole*. What more could we ask for than a life where we whisper His name with every breath?

As the morning light crept into their room, Priscilla smiled and kissed her sweet Aquila on the cheek.

"Wake up," she said quietly. "The world is waiting to hear His name."

His eyes opened and focused on his lovely bride, the woman he had walked many miles and days with.

"Good morning," he answered sweetly, reaching for his clothes. No more fig leaves, no more shame. Just a man and a woman who knew they had been chosen, just as you have.

Your life, your voice, and your heart—they were given purpose before the foundations of the world were laid. And it is all for this great King Jesus, who speaks to you now as He did to Priscilla and Aquila then.

Did you know that your life is a part of this same story? The story that stretches from the beginning of time into the farthest tomorrow? It is. I assure you. And if you listen carefully, in every moment, you can still hear Him.

"Go, Love, and be brave. Speak My name to all who will listen. . . . After all, you have been chosen for such a time as this."

—FROM ACTS 18; ROMANS 16

He

God is made up of three persons: Father, Son, and Spirit. This is called the **trinity**. God the Father, Jesus Christ the Son of God, and the Holy Spirit are all distinct persons of the same God. They have different jobs, but each person is fully God. It's hard for us to imagine how the three persons of God could be different and yet the same, but it's another part of God's mystery that our minds just can't fully hold.

Me

Do you think God wants you to slam your doors and keep people away from the home He has given you? He doesn't! He wants you to share it with other people, making it a safe place for them to come and rest and learn more about Him. Think about some ways you could invite neighbors or friends over and make them feel welcome and loved by God. When you do this, you are being hospitable, which is a wonderful way to tell God that you care about taking care of others.

She

Lord, give _____ a desire and a willingness to be hospitable (1 Peter 4:9), remembering that You have commanded us to be good stewards of all You have given us. Help me make our home a haven where people who don't know You are able to sense You and those who do are able to rest and be in Your presence. Remind me that it doesn't have to look perfect or be worthy of a magazine cover to be a refuge for others, and help me identify the ways I can invite the kingdom closer by opening my doors and my life to others.

Philoxenos (fil OX en os) is the Greek word for "hospitality."
The memory verse for this story is Acts 18:26—
"He began to speak boldly in the synagogue. After Priscilla and Aquila heard him,
they took him home and explained the way of God to him more accurately."

A Peek Behind the Scenes

—from Angie Smith

As a mom to daughters, I have longed for a story-book Bible that focused on women in Scripture, and I'm so excited to be a part of this one. From the beginning, it felt like a special project but also a project with a lot of responsibility. I wanted to choose language and story-telling that will appeal to children, but it was imperative to make it biblically accurate.

Our vision was to create a storybook Bible that was relatable, accessible, and educational to girls, allowing them to see themselves in the characters of God's Word and to be made more aware of the high calling we have been given as His daughters. Although it is not a complete retelling of all the major stories in Scripture, we did try to maintain the over-arching storyline of the Bible in the wonderful (and not-so-wonderful!) women we chose to include.

By including the devotional sections at the end of each story, we hope we've given a tangible, practical way to apply the truths presented in the stories. Our prayer is that mothers and fathers will sit with their daughters and read these words, and as a result, their girls will be led to the very words of God.

And who knows whether you have not come to the kingdom for such a time as this?
~ Esther 4:14 (ESV)

DAY 2

DAY 2

DAY 3

DAY 4

DAY 5

DAY 6

Angie and I decided to alternate between color and black and white drawings, incorporating a unique, sketchy style we both loved.
—Breezy

Your people shall be my people, and your god my god. ~Ruth 1:16 (ESV)

Having worked on another book with Breezy in the past (*Audrey Bunny*), we knew one another pretty well, and more than that, we loved and appreciated one another in a way that is virtually unheard of in the publishing world. More often than not, the illustrator and the author aren't in contact very much throughout the process, and the publisher of the book acts as a liaison of sorts. In this case, it was so obvious that the Lord had brought us together that B&H smiled, gave us their blessing, and allowed us to truly co-labor as we went.

We would send each other text messages, emails, or phone calls of prayer, asking one another what the focus was that day, and just generally approaching the project as a team. It never failed that I would write something, send it along, and then see her illustrations bring my words to life. It is a rare gift we have in one another—and one neither of us takes for granted.

We knew from the outset that what mattered most to us was telling biblically accurate stories that would inspire girls, and we made that our priority. I spent hours and hours reading Scripture, simply letting the words soak in while asking the Lord for wisdom on how to write the story in a way that was appropriate for the age group we were focusing on. Many times I had commentaries stacked around me like I was a seminary student, and I found myself giggling at how long I spent agonizing over word choices and whether or not to include certain details. I had a fantastic editor (thank you, Amy!) who made sure to shape up the stories in beautiful ways, and then several other people looked over each story to make sure it was theologically sound.

Where Scripture is silent, there should be great caution in making assumptions, and in the incidences where dialogue or ideas were included here, it was in ways that didn't compromise the Bible's account or the integrity of the text itself.

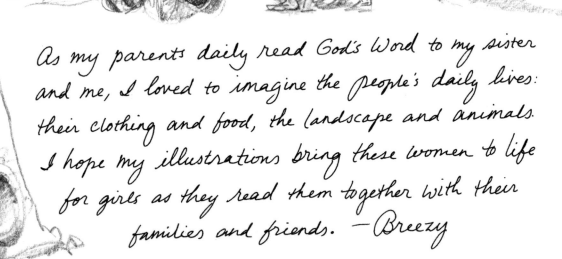

As my parents daily read God's Word to my sister and me, I loved to imagine the people's daily lives: their clothing and food, the landscape and animals. I hope my illustrations bring these women to life for girls as they read them together with their families and friends. —Breezy

Even before the writing began, we made a decision not to ever show the face of Christ in the illustrations. He is simply too wonderful, too magnificent, too mysterious and holy and perfect to try and depict His face. There is a trembling in our hearts as we even try to do what wc have done here, but the idea of presuming our humble, unsteady human hands could possibly portray Him? It is holy ground, and ground neither of us dared to tread. You will see His feet, His hands, or the back of His head, but we wanted there to be an appropriate amount of mystery when it came to His face.

Even before the writing began, we made the decision not to ever show the face of Christ in the illustrations.

From Concept to Illustration

—from Breezy Brookshire

As I started the illustrations for this book, I read Angie's stories and the accounts in Scripture, sketching my ideas as they came to mind.

They started as thumbnails, which are small sketches that help me lay out everything in the picture. After choosing the best thumbnails, I emailed them to Angie and the publishing team for their feedback. With their approval, I would proceed to the final watercolor or pencil drawing.

The pencil drawings were made with a variety of hard and soft pencils, giving me a broad range of light and dark lines to work with.

1. *Thumbnails*

2. *Drawing*

3. *Painting*

Each painting started as a light pencil drawing. Then I began to carefully paint; the colors, lights, and shadows. And slowly, by the grace of God, it would become a finished watercolor.

When I finished a watercolor or drawing, I emailed an image of it to the publishing team for approval. I handed it to my sister Emily Rose who then carefully scanned and prepared it for the publisher.

Designing the look of each woman was a weighty but delightful responsibility. I often turned to my collection of reference material (photographs, examples of traditional clothing, maps, historians' research, and Scripture itself) to help me convey their personalities, to illustrate what would have existed at that time, and ultimately to point to the Creator who designed it all.

"He is not here, but has risen!"
—Luke 24:6 (ESV)

The Inner
Tunic

The Outer
Tunic

The Cloak
or Mantle

The Priestly
Garments

Shoes or
Sandals

Men's
Clothing

The
Headdress

The Israelites' clothing was simple and made
of wool or flax, and designs could be woven
into the fabric. They wore headdresses often
to protect themselves from the sun.

The Inner Tunic

The Outer Tunic

The Cloak

Women's Clothing

Shoes or Sandals

The Belt or Girdle

The Headdress

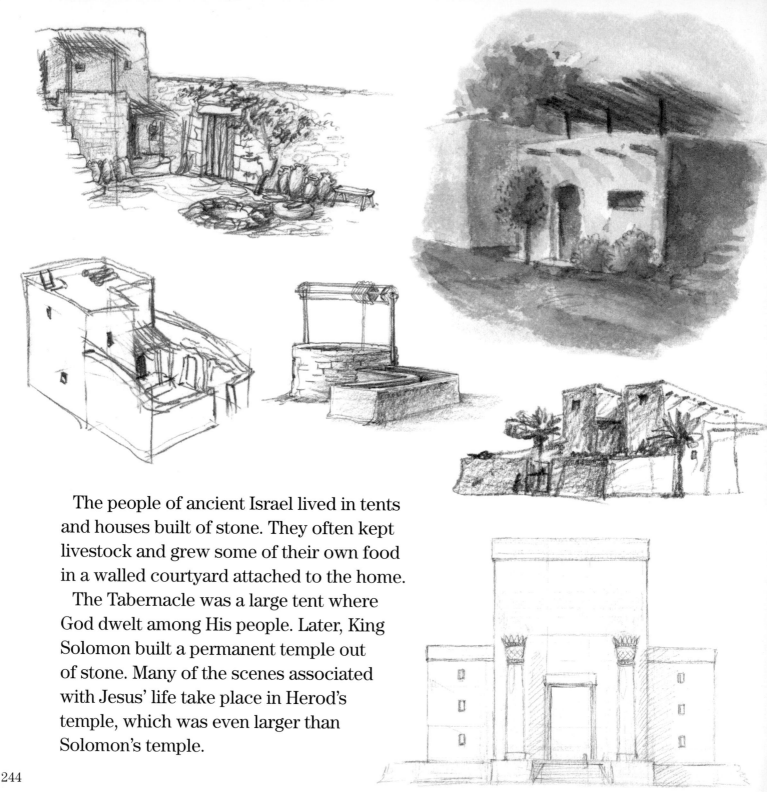

The people of ancient Israel lived in tents and houses built of stone. They often kept livestock and grew some of their own food in a walled courtyard attached to the home.

The Tabernacle was a large tent where God dwelt among His people. Later, King Solomon built a permanent temple out of stone. Many of the scenes associated with Jesus' life take place in Herod's temple, which was even larger than Solomon's temple.

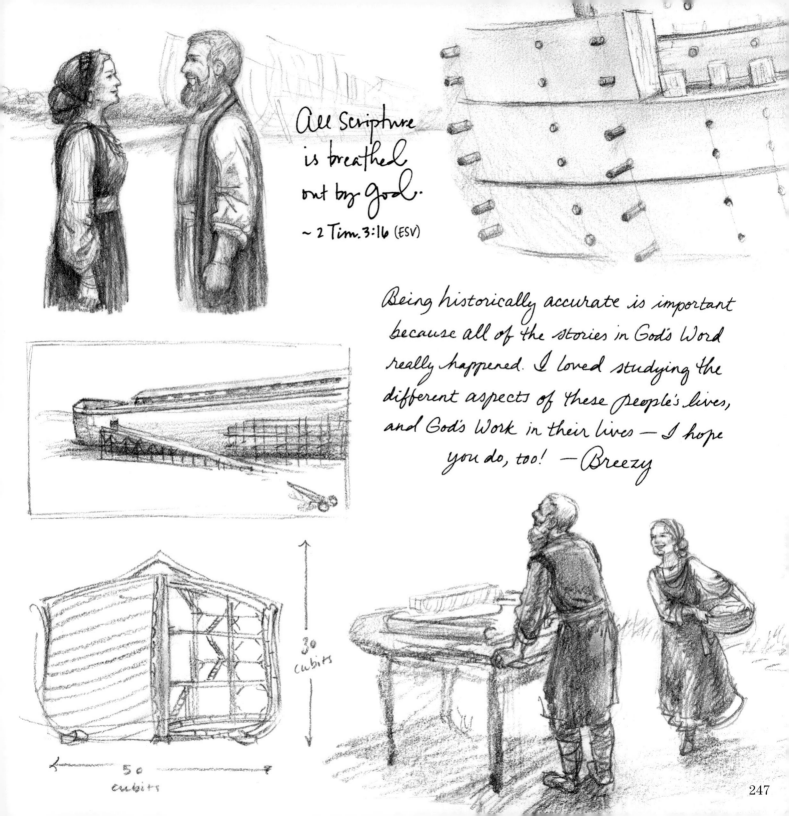

All Scripture is breathed out by god.

~ 2 Tim. 3:16 (ESV)

Being historically accurate is important because all of the stories in God's Word really happened. I loved studying the different aspects of these people's lives, and God's Work in their lives — I hope you do, too! —Breezy

30 cubits

50 cubits

Daughter, your faith has made you well; go in peace.
~ Luke 8:48 (ESV)

Charm is deceitful and beauty is vain, but a woman who fears the Lord is to be praised.
~ Prov. 31:30 (ESV)

For Such a Time as This

For Such a Time as This

The Lord is my light and my salvation; whom shall I fear?
~ Ps. 27:1 (ESV)

249

Also Available from Angie Smith

"I chose you, Audrey, and I love you more than you could ever know."

Looking out from a barrel of stuffed animals at the toyshop, Audrey Bunny is afraid her imperfections make her unworthy of being chosen to receive a little girl's love. She'll learn the truth soon enough, and young readers will learn that everyone is special and wonderfully made by God.

Available everywhere books are sold.

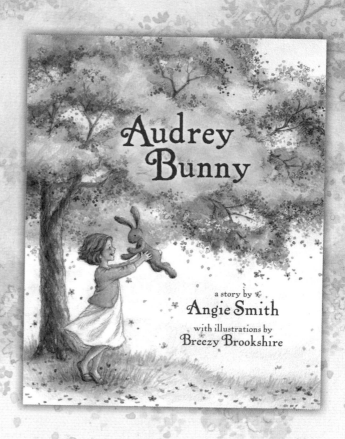

Audrey Bunny

a story by
Angie Smith

with illustrations by
Breezy Brookshire

Also Available from Angie Smith

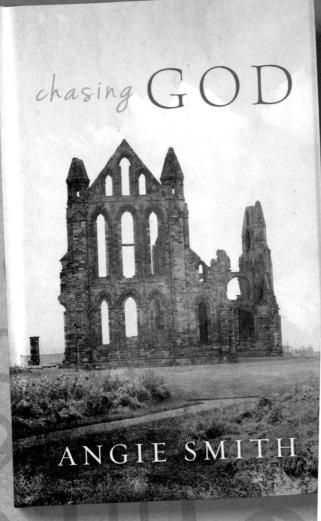

chasing GOD

ANGIE SMITH

#ChasingGod

So many requirements, so many rules, and so much guilt where there is supposed to be freedom. It's the reason you wonder if you've measured up, and the nagging voice that tells you you're a failure as a Christian. Three simple words changed everything for Angie Smith, and she believes they can do the same for you.

STOP CHASING GOD.

B&H
Every WORD Matters®
BHPublishingGroup.com